Successful
Application
of Quality Systems
in K–12 Schools

Also Available from ASQ Quality Press:

Improving Student Learning: Applying Deming's Quality Principles in Classrooms
Lee Jenkins

Futuring Tools for Strategic Quality Planning in Education
William F. Alexander and Richard W. Serfass

Living on the Edge of Chaos: Leading Schools into the Global Age
Karolyn J. Snyder, Michel Acker-Hocevar, and Kristen M. Snyder

Insights to Performance Excellence in Education: An Inside Look at the Baldrige Award Criteria for Education
Mark L. Blazey, Karen S. Davison, and John P. Evans

Orchestrating Learning with Quality
David P. Langford and Barbara Cleary

Tools and Techniques to Inspire Classroom Learning
Barbara A. Cleary, Ph.D. and Sally J. Duncan

Thinking Tools for Kids: An Activity Book for Classroom Learning
Barbara A. Cleary, Ph.D. and Sally J. Duncan

Self-Assessment Guide to Performance Excellence: Aligning Your School with the 2001 Malcolm Baldrige Criteria for Performance Excellence
Koalaty Kid

To request a complimentary catalog of ASQ Quality Press publications, call 800-248-1946, or visit our website at http://qualitypress.asq.org .

Successful Application of Quality Systems in K–12 Schools

The Education Division
of the
American Society for Quality
In cooperation with
ASQ Koalaty Kid

American Society for Quality
Milwaukee, Wisconsin

Library of Congress Cataloging-in-Publication Data

Successful applications of quality systems in K–12 schools / F. Craig Johnson, Robert Kattman, editors.

    p. cm.

"The Education Division of the American Society for Quality in cooperation with ASQ Koalaty Kid."

Includes bibliographical references and index.

  ISBN 0-87389-565-7 (pbk.)

  1. Educational accountability--United States--Case studies. 2. School improvement programs--United States--Case studies. I. Johnson, F. Craig. II. Kattman, Robert. III. American Society for Quality. Education Division. IV. American Society for Quality. Koalaty Kid.

  LB2806.22 .S83 2003

  371.2'00973--dc21

2002011696

10 9 8 7 6 5 4 3 2 1

ISBN 0-87389-565-7

Publisher: William A. Tony
Acquisitions Editor: Annemieke Koudstaal
Project Editor: Craig S. Powell
Production Administrator: Gretchen Trautman
Special Marketing Representative: David Luth

ASQ Mission: The American Society for Quality advances individual, organizational and community excellence worldwide through learning, quality improvement and knowledge exchange.

Attention: Bookstores, Wholesalers, Schools and Corporations:
ASQ Quality Press books, videotapes, audiotapes, and software are available at quantity discounts with bulk purchases for business, educational, or instructional use. For information, please contact ASQ Quality Press at 800-248-1946, or write to ASQ Quality Press, P.O. Box 3005, Milwaukee, WI 53201-3005.

To place orders or to request a free copy of the ASQ Quality Press Publications Catalog, including ASQ membership information, call 800-248-1946. Visit our Web site at http://www.asq.org .

Printed in the United States of America

 Printed on acid-free paper

American Society for Quality

ASQ

Quality Press
600 N. Plankinton Avenue
Milwaukee, Wisconsin 53203
Call toll free 800-248-1946
Fax 414-272-1734
www.asq.org
http://qualitypress.asq.org
http://standardsgroup.asq.org
E-mail: authors@asq.org

Dedicated to Frank Caplan, without whom there would be no book, for his guidance during the year of chapter development and for his editing of the final draft.

Table of Contents

Chapter 1 Data-based Decisions

Lee Jenkins

Chapter 2 Process

Suzanne Keely

Chapter 5 Empowering the People

Dr. William N. Kiefer

Chapter 6 Utilizing Partnerships

Robert Kattman

Chapter 7 Continual Improvement

Grant Smith

Chapter 8 Systems in K–12 Schools
Frank Caplan

Preface

The successful applications of quality systems in K–12 schools (hereafter "schools") described in this book applied the principles found in the following publications:

Malcolm Baldrige National Quality Award—*Education Criteria for Performance Excellence*

ASQ Koalaty Kid—*Self-Assessment Guide to Performance Excellence*

ASQ Z1.11-2002, Guidelines for the Application of ANSI/ISO/ASQ Q9001-2000 to Education and Training Institutions

These principles form a framework to interrelate the school's curricular criteria, performance standards, supporting tools, evaluation methods, and corrective actions. The authors learned that principles needed to support each other. If one or more principles was not followed, then energy was diverted into nonproductive activity. The school's effectiveness was reduced with no identifiable benefit. The authors came to appreciate a complete system that integrated all their quality management system elements.

One reviewer advised the authors to target the book to the educational practitioners who want an easy-to-read cookbook on how-to-do-it. The authors did not take this advice. This book is not an easy-read cookbook with flavor-of-the-month recipes. It gives few how-to instructions. The authors played leadership roles as school district superintendents, school principals, curriculum directors, curriculum coordinators, and consultants from professional societies. They spent many hours doing the extra work required, were often discouraged, and sometimes had to start over. It took a long time—typically a decade. Half of the decade was spent revising the curriculum into requirements with measurable objectives. Concurrently, quality tools were being applied to improve school services. The second five years were spent following the quality systems guidelines cited above. There were no shortcuts and no quick fixes, only many hours of hard work and some frustration. They took time to find the critical factors necessary for successful quality systems. They understood the continuing need for the school board's support throughout the long development process and routinely reported on what worked and what was continuing to work for their schools. The decade was anything but easy.

Why did they do it? Why should others be encouraged to follow them? The simplest and most common answer was, "Because it worked for us." The major benefits were that students learned more effectively, teachers were empowered to do what they were trained to do, administrators and staff found the courage to accept responsibility for problems, to describe and monitor processes, to identify problems, to establish metrics, to collect data, and to allocate resources to support the learning process. They found that a credible quality system discouraged "tinkering" with the school system and empowered the school's people to face problems and to solve them. They found they saved time preparing for accreditation renewals because much of data collected for the quality management system satisfied the requirements of other accreditation bodies.

Finally, all eight chapters describe quality management systems operating in different schools. The chapters can be read in any order. These are real-life, not idealized, examples. Repetition of key elements in different chapters is to be expected and may reinforce each other.

Each chapter focuses on one of the eight internationally accepted quality principles. They are not prescriptions. They describe one way of applying the principle in a school in the words of the school administrators who led the application. Many others contributed to the development of the quality management systems and are acknowledged below.

ACKNOWLEDGEMENTS

The following people have been identified by the chapter authors as administrators, teachers, and others who have made significant contributions to the development of the quality management systems described in this book.

Superintendents

Tom Armelino—Enterprise School District, Redding, California

John G. Conyer—CCSD #15—The Palatine School District, Illinois

Tom Lamers—Liberty Center Schools, Liberty Center, Ohio

Vicki Phillips—School District of Lancaster, Lancaster, Pennsylvania

Perry Soldwedel—Pekin Public Schools District 108, Pekin, Illinois

Fred Susor—Penta Career Center, Perrysburg, Ohio

Winona Winn—Turner School District, Kansas City, Kansas

Principals

Allan Amos—Junction Elementary School, Kansas City, Kansas

Pam Cullotta—Avon School, Grayslake, Illinois

Darlene G. Davis—Conshohocken Elementary School, Conshohocken, Pennsylvania

David Sanders—Mark Twain Elementary School, Richardson, Texas

Mary Jo Taylor—Ridgeview Elementary School, Ashtabula, Ohio

Rick Utz—Liberty Center High School, Liberty Center, Ohio

Leota Youngblood—Horace Mann Elementary School, Shawnee, Oklahoma

School Administrators and Curriculum Coordinators

Philip Bufton—Curriculum Specialist, Glendale-River Hills Schools, Milwaukee, Wisconsin

Kevin Whitlatch—Director, Penta Career Center, Adult & Continuing Education, Perrysburg , Ohio

Teachers

Carolyn Ayres—Alta Mesa School, Enterprise School District, Redding, California

Jeff Burgard—Science, Chrysalis School, Redding, California

Sandra Buss—Sterling Morton Elementary School, Mentor, Ohio

Shelly Carson—History and Social Science, Foothill High School, Palo Cedro, California

Pat Channell—Center Street Elementary School, Mentor, Ohio

Boni Cooper—Reynolds Elementary School, Mentor, Ohio

Laurel Deiss—Sterling Morton Elementary School, Mentor, Ohio

Laurie Eppler—Sterling Morton Elementary School, Mentor, Ohio

Karen Fauss—Boulder Creek School, Enterprise School District, Redding, California

Betty Gordon—Jefferson Elementary School, Willoughby, Ohio

Denise Hoover—Sterling Morton Elementary School, Mentor, Ohio

DeAnn Isaksen—North Madison Elementary School, Madison, Ohio

Marion Lipinski—Center Street Elementary School, Mentor, Ohio

Christina Redford—Center Street Elementary School, Mentor, Ohio

Julia McLeod—North Madison Elementary School, Madison, Ohio

Dianna Misich—Homer Nash Kimbell Elementary School, Madison, Ohio

Vicki Oliver—Redbird Elementary School, Madison, Ohio

Dave Rogaliner—Redbird Elementary School, Madison, Ohio

Jill Ryerson—Reynolds Elementary School, Mentor, Ohio

Susan Stauffer—Sterling Morton Elementary School, Mentor, Ohio

Nadine Westerdahl—Headlands Elementary School, Mentor, Ohio

Vivian Young—Sterling Morton Elementary School, Mentor, Ohio

State Government Agencies and Consultants

Brad Carleton—Consultant, Ohio Department of Education, Adult Workforce Development, Columbus, Ohio

Richard Haines—Diversified Industrial Training Coordinator, Polaris Career Center, Ohio

Barbara Nichol—Associate Director, Ohio Department of Education, Adult Workforce Development, Columbus, Ohio

Publishers

Marcel Dekker for permission to reproduce portions of F. Craig Johnson and Grant S. Smith's, "Process Stability and Process Capability in Public Schools," *Quality Engineering* 9, no. 3 (1997): 503–520.

Editors

F. Craig Johnson chairs the ASQ Education Division and Robert Kattman is Immediate Past Chair. (See page 109.) Craig also chairs the ASQ/ANSI Task Group for Education, which developed the education standard ASQ Z1.11-2002. He works with other ISO delegates to develop terms and definitions relating to quality management standards.

Introduction

This book covers classroom quality management and quality management of school support services. Some of these terms need to be defined for use in schools.

Quality in schools means the degree to which measurable learning characteristics are consistent with curriculum objectives.

Measurable learning characteristics include intelligence, memory, knowledge, skills, and attitude, among others.

Curriculum objectives come from needs and expectations of parents, government regulations, and the cultural values of society.

Quality management of school support services means the degree to which school service requirements are met. These requirements cover the safety and well-being of students, the effective conduct of the administrative responsibilities, and conformity to regulations.

Quality management systems require school administrators to establish measures of "how well" requirements assure students, parents, the school board, and the general public that everything in the school works as it was designed to work. For more, see

http://www.iso.ch/iso/en/iso9000-14000/iso9000/qmp.html

Registration to ISO 9000 generally involves having an accredited independent third party conduct an on-site audit of your school's operations against the requirements of the appropriate standard.

Standards can be requirements like ISO 9001, criteria like the Baldrige, or guidelines like ISO 9004. They range from "basic" like ISO 9001 to "excellence" like Baldrige.

EIGHT QUALITY PRINCIPLES

Quality principles provide a realistic framework for schools to develop a successful quality management system. Eight quality principles are used in this book with examples from existing quality management systems in K–12 schools. There is no hierarchy or development sequence implied by the order of the chapters, which can be read in any order.

PRINCIPLE 1—Information and Analysis

Improvement begins with reliable measurements. The measurements are simpler for maintaining consistent learning and support processes than are measurements for solving problems. Teachers, staff, and administrators want to know how often events occur and use measures of *frequency* displayed as graphs (see Figures 1.6 through 1.8). Sometimes they want to monitor the *variability* in the performance of an entire class (see Figure 1.1) or of an individual student (see Figure 1.3). On occasion the school is interested in *relationships* (see Figure 1.2). Often there is interest in monitoring the order of the steps in a process (see Figure 2.5). These displays, called histograms, control charts, scatter diagrams, and flowcharts are available in inexpensive software packages. They are simple displays that ease the burden of monitoring and recording performance. The California experience, as told in chapter 1 by Lee Jenkins, found that a quality-related learning process included control limits, performance measures, and demographic data. The most useful data were reliable, consistent, standardized, timely, current, accurate, and available. For the purposes of analysis, data needed to include records of comparisons, benchmarks, and reports of evaluations. The analysis was most effective when numerical information, results, and performance dimensions were presented as graphs that teachers used for providing feedback to students.

PRINCIPLE 2—Process Management

All work is made up of processes. A process has a beginning and an end. During that time it changes the value of a metric to form an output. This could be illustrated by a student who enters first grade knowing how to spell a few three-letter words correctly. After planned lessons, drill, testing, and practice, the student can spell more and longer words correctly. If errors are frequent, then some enriched activity may be appropriate. Learning is achieved more effectively when resources and activities are related to the learning process. Schools with a successful quality system assure consistent processes with a continuing monitoring of student performance related to the curriculum and the supporting services that enable effective learning. Process effectiveness, as documented by Suzanne Keely in chapter 2 from her experience with Koalaty Kid schools, was found to change the value of permanent characteristics as ignorance became knowledge, disobedience became conformity, and children became young adults. Actions within school processes often interact with each other just as processes within a school system interact with each other.

PRINCIPLE 3—Leadership

Leaders establish unity of purpose and direction. Leadership was a critical function for schools with a mature quality system if they wished to implement and maintain an internationally recognized and proven quality management system. Leadership in an Ohio school, as reported by Judith Zaczkowski in chapter 3, created a consistent purpose in teaching, policies, curriculum, and development for teaching reading. The different management styles among school districts were not a factor in the effectiveness of the quality management system. Senior leaders in a school system set directions within an accepted value system. Senior leaders encouraged participation in quality improvement at all levels and served as role models for quality of life and continuous emphasis on quality in all things. Senior leaders provided systematic and documented best reading practice and systematic improvement of school processes, and took responsibility for maintaining the value of assets.

PRINCIPLE 4—Student and Stakeholder Focus

Schools should understand students' needs and stakeholders' expectations. Schools developed public confidence, as Joe Thomas observed in chapter 4, by meeting student learning objectives and, in the process, exceeding the community's expectations. Community members did not visit schools very often but, when they did, they expected to find the same service provided that they experienced in any retail or service organization. For these reasons, K–12 schools with a quality system reached out into their communities with surveys to determine the community's requirements and expectations. The example in chapter 4 found that students, while not customers in the usual sense, were seen by the community as the primary beneficiaries of education and, in that context, were considered as customers in the quality system. The secondary beneficiaries (interested parties) included parents, higher education, the marketplace, and society in general and the relationships among them are more manageable when common needs are identified and understood as a part of the quality system.

PRINCIPLE 5—Empowering Teachers and Staff

Employees, at all levels, are the essence of public schools, and their full involvement enables effective use of quality teams, tools, and technology to improve the school's effectiveness and efficiency. In the Lancaster, Pennsylvania story, as told by Bill Kiefer in chapter 5, teachers, staff, and administrators were considered assets that provide and maintain the schools' intellectual capital. They were closest to a school process and were more likely to understand it. They studied school processes systematically and improved them. These improved school processes reduced waste and motivated additional process improvements. As these schools are registered to ISO 9001, there is independent verification of the results achieved.

PRINCIPLE 6—Partnerships

Community organizations and suppliers can provide independent and mutually beneficial relationships that enhance the ability to create value. In the Wisconsin schools, described by Robert Kattman in chapter 6, the school district established strategic alliances or partnerships with a regional laboratory, ensuring early involvement and participation in defining the requirements for joint development and improvement of products, processes, and systems. They developed mutual trust, respect, and commitment to customer satisfaction and continual improvement.

PRINCIPLE 7—Continual Process Improvement

Improvement in processes and results should be a permanent objective of schools. A curriculum specifies what students are expected to learn and how their learning is to be assessed. Grant Smith made a study of an alternative school in Florida. His results in chapter 7 showed that the curriculum, by itself, did not guarantee that students' needs and expectations would be understood if the processes were not in control. Once this was recognized by the school administrators, deficient administrative practices were replaced by the application of standards and associated guidelines when implementing a quality system within K–12 schools. School improvement became a continuing goal of each school. When that was the case, results continued to rise and costs continued to fall.

PRINCIPLE 8—System Perspective

The quality system perspective comes from identifying, understanding, and managing schools as a system of interrelated processes. As pointed out by Frank Caplan in chapter 8, each quality system is influenced by different objectives, by different instructional methods, and by different administrative practices specific to the school. An example of this comes from Florida, where seven quality systems in seven school districts were quite different in implementation. The quality system that worked best was the simplest one for the special character of each school. Generally, in schools with effective quality systems, students did not fail but the quality system failed to understand the students' needs. These system failures were the responsibility of administrators who operated the quality system and were empowered to solve quality problems. The failures could be turned into successes when all information was identified and documented so all the necessary system elements could function together.

1

Data-based Decisions

Lee Jenkins

INTRODUCTION

"How's my Mary doing in school?" asks the parent. This simple question is at the heart of a quality management system in schools. The parent did not ask about teachers, curriculum, schedules, facilities, or resources, but rather about "how well" one student is doing. It is a customer's question on quality. The information needed to answer this question is difficult to collect and summarize without a well-defined system of interrelated or interacting data collection processes. Such a system is commonly known as a quality management system for a school. In these schools, the teacher is able to give an answer to the parent based on regular, reliable, and valid measurements of a student's performance. Without these data, the teacher can give only general, subjective, and incomplete answers to the parent's question—satisfying neither the parent nor the teacher.

In addition, schools with well-managed quality systems in place enable teachers to relate learning objectives to individual success and test results to individual learning problems. Individual performance results can be related to peer groups, to school's standards, and to national testing norms. Teachers can provide specific steps the school and parents can take to make the learning process more effective. Both the parent and the teacher gain confidence in the processes that lead to better results.

The community is assured that appropriate subject matter for children and adolescents is being taught in order for students to be successful. Quality system elements work together to assure that the school's employees, facilities, equipment, processes, and information systems are directed toward achieving common objectives of student learning. Needs and expectations of parents, school board members, local businesses, the professional community, the state legislatures, and society as a whole are translated into requirements for students. All interested parties are assured that the school's records system contains data on each student's performance related to these requirements and that those schools are assets that will continue to produce value for schoolchildren.

The following example illustrates the way the quality system is expressed in a parent conference. Each teacher is prepared to present data to the parent in answer to the question, "How's my Mary doing in school?" Data are in the form of easy to read graphs that can be adapted to a parent's question while the conference is in progress. The parent leaves the conference confident that the school knows where Mary stands academically at this time and has a plan to take necessary steps to assure Mary's continuing progress.

Mary has mastered 38 of the 70 course objectives at the half-way point of this school year. She is moving along with her classmates, and has a positive attitude toward school. While Mary understands word problems and can identify several appropriate methods for each problem, she needs to work on her measurement and geometry as she cannot visualize the concepts. Increasing the number of measurement and geometry activities, plus having more math conversations, should correct this by the end of the school year. If not, we might want to discuss the summer program designed to assist students with gaps in meeting standards. We can talk about this at the next conference.

(Figures 1.3 and 1.5, later in this chapter, are examples of the graphs the teacher is sharing with Mary's parents in this meeting.)

A quality management system can also assist support service processes in K–12 schools. The quality systems approach is illustrated in the following description of procedures used to order materials from the warehouse before and after a quality management system was in place in the Volusia School System in Florida.

In the immature system there was a three week cycle. When orders were placed at the beginning of the cycle, the supplies might arrive in as little as one month. If the order missed the cycle, it could take two or three months. If the items were not on backorder, the time cycle would begin again with the same delay time. The warehouse staff began to improve their quality system on their own by visiting a successful commercial warehouse. Within a year, the quality system had matured to the point where if a teacher placed an order before 3 PM it would be delivered by 10 AM the next day. Teachers consulted an online backorder list before ordering. In the immature system, the annual December audit closed down the warehouse for two weeks for inventory. In the mature system, the entire warehouse stock was audited by closing time each day. Auditors were welcome anytime.

DECISION-MAKING APPROACHES

Fear-based Decisions

Everyone wants improved student learning. The students do. The educators do. Business leaders do. And government leaders pass laws to increase student learning. Each of the groups decides that the best way to make improvements in student learning is to treat the people organizationally below them exactly how they don't want to be treated by the people organizationally above them. So, these groups add more fear to the lives of those they deem responsible for the lack of student learning. Legislators add more fear to the lives of school administrators, school administrators add more fear to the lives of teachers, and teachers add more fear to the lives of students. Students rebel.

Bribery-based Decisions

A second approach for improved learning is bribery. Usually this is in tandem with fear. Quite simply the approach is to bring about improvement based on objective data and analysis. If you improve, life will be wonderful; but if you don't improve, you will feel fear and pain. Sometimes, however, the fear part is not added. It is quite simply that the school, teacher, or student who wins the educational contest gets a big reward. All other schools, teachers, and students are, by default, loser schools, loser teachers, and loser students.

Blame-based Decisions

The third theory for improvement is blame. Somehow people believe that blaming people will cause them to desire to improve. Twenty great families give up an evening for a September back-to-school night, for example, only to hear the teacher blame the other 10 families for their "lack of caring." No group involved in educational issues has avoided using blame as a means of improvement. Teachers, administrators, parents, journalists, legislators, business leaders, and ministers have all used this approach.

Novelty-based Decisions

The fourth theory for improvement is to purchase the latest, greatest educational program and mandate its use. Surely, somebody in another state is smarter than us. We will buy their program and make everybody use it.

Data-based Decisions

The fifth approach is based upon quality principles. Everyone in the organization looks at the same data screens. At the very least, those in power treat the people organizationally below them the way they want to be treated. Teams study data to determine the best approach for improved student learning, carry out the plans, and then study the data to see if improvement has occurred. The teams are:

- School board members and their superintendent
- The superintendent and school administrators
- Principals and teachers
- Teachers and their students
- A teacher, a student, and parents

Obviously there are other combinations for team making, but the point is that everybody is a member of a team, has equal access to data, and analyzes the data for leadership toward a constant purpose.

How then do students and teachers know exactly the learning taking place in their classrooms on a regular basis?

This chapter provides one method. The sequence of events follows:

1. Students are provided at the beginning of a course the information and performance levels expected at the end of the course. For illustrative purposes, let's assume there are 100 concepts or items to be learned in the course.
2. Each week students are quizzed on a sample from the whole course. Thus students may be quizzed on items not to be taught until May during the first quiz in September. The square root of the information to be learned is an adequate sample size. In this example the square root of 100 is 10, so 10 items are randomly selected each week from the total 100. Each time an item reappears in a later weekly quiz, the question illuminating that item is different from the previous one(s) for that item.
3. Graphs are prepared for both students and teachers from the quiz data. These graphs are for the purpose of giving insight into what should occur to improve learning.

It has been the experience of the writer that students are willing to work hard to improve both the classroom graphs and individual graphs. The feedback that their hard work is paying off is much more important to them than either avoidance of pain (stick) or gaining of reward (carrot).

A CONVERSATION

The retelling of a conversation with a 7th grader is probably the best summary of these steps.

Jenkins: Tell me, are any of your teachers giving a weekly quiz—sort of a silly one—with graphs being made each week from the results?

Student: Yes, in science.

Jenkins: How does it work?

Student: Well, my teacher gave us a list of 100 important science facts to be learned this year. Each week we have a quiz on 10 of the 100.

Jenkins: How does the quiz work?

Student: My teacher has some dice that look like a golf ball. They have 100 numbers on them. The kids take turns rolling a die to see what concepts we'll be tested on.

Jenkins: So, you don't know exactly which items are going to be on the quiz the day ahead?

Student: No.

Jenkins: What happens next?

Student: The teacher asks us the 10 questions and we correct the tests. The teacher gathers up the tests from us kids. She then adds up the total correct.

Jenkins: The total correct? She wants to know how many all of you kids answered all together.

Student: Yes.

Jenkins: How are you doing?

Student: Three weeks ago we answered 269 questions correctly.

Jenkins: Was that a good week?

Student: Yes, it was our best week ever. There are 32 students in our classroom, so we correctly answered 269 out of 320 questions.

Jenkins: What happens when you have a good week?

Student: My teacher is *really* happy.

Jenkins: Have you had bad weeks?

Student: Yes, one week we only answered 72 questions correctly. That was a bad luck week—a lot of people were sick plus the questions were all really hard.

Jenkins: Do you know personally how you are doing?

Student: Yes, each student makes graphs of his or her own tests. The teacher makes the graph of the class, but we have to make the graph for our own little tests.

Jenkins: Are you happy with your progress?

Student: Yes, I'm answering eight or nine a week now.

Jenkins: So, what do the kids think of this crazy way to give tests?

Student: They like it. They won't let the teacher ever forget to give the weekly test.

The two types of data for educators to study are results data and process data. Typically, results data in education are year-end results from final testing. They are presented to educators in the form of pages and pages of averages. There is not much one can do with an average except feel guilty, celebrate, blame, or threaten.

For example, suppose a class is tested on 100 science questions. The average student misses 26.76 questions at year's end. What can a teacher do with this information? Not a lot.

On the other hand, suppose the teacher has a histogram of the results. The histogram shows three students with 0–5 errors, 10 with 6–10 errors, one with 11–15 errors, three with 16–20 errors, and 13 with over 50 errors. The improvement goal for the following year is quite simply to have fewer students with over 50 errors and more students with fewer than 10 errors. This view of the classroom can energize a teacher and the students whereas the average does almost nothing.

The problems of the average are further exacerbated if each of the science teachers gives the same exam and the averages from the five classrooms are ranked and posted. In place of ranked averages, educators need histograms for classrooms, schools, school districts, and states.

Even though results data can be displayed in histograms rather than ranked averages, at least educators have a history of results data. When it comes to process data, however, education has had none. In 1992 at a seminar sponsored by the American Association of School Administrators, Dr. W. Edwards Deming described a process for teachers to use in collecting process data. Educators have found the process effective for managing both the learning of information and performance.

ANALYSIS OF DATA

Dr. Deming's suggestion was for teachers to determine the information to be known at the end of the course. Students, for example, could be expected to learn 100 essential science facts at the end of sixth grade. During the first week of school students are provided a list of the 100 essential facts (no trivia) and are given a quiz on 10 of the 100 facts. Dr. Deming suggested that each week students be quizzed on the square root of the total content on items randomly selected. He then suggested that the total number of questions answered correctly by the whole class would be posted for the teacher and students to study (see Figure 1.1). The figures that follow are from a 6th grade science class that has completed 75 percent of the 2001–2002 school year.

Dr. Deming further suggested that the teacher have a scatter diagram prepared each week with a dot for each student. *Class Action* software (see resources) was written by Blackthorne Publishing of Miami, FL to make this dot production available to teachers instantly. Figure 1.2 is the scatter diagram that corresponds to the run chart in Figure 1.1.

On the computer screen the teacher can point to any dot and the name of the student will appear on the screen. Further, the dots can be printed in color, disaggregated by gender, ethnicity, or any other variable

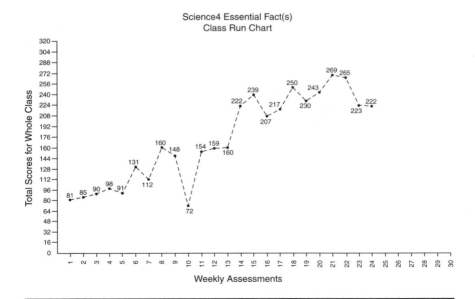

Figure 1.1 Class run chart.

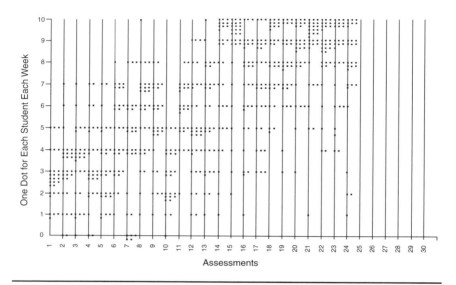

Figure 1.2 Class scatter diagram.

of interest. The scatter diagram, along with the run chart, provides the teacher with complete process data for managing learning.

When students have the class run chart shown in Figure 1.1 and their individual student run chart shown in Figure 1.3, they almost automatically see that learning can be managed without fear, bribery, blame, or prepackaged curriculum. They are eager to share with the teacher suggestions that will cause the graph to go up.

Recently a second grader was asked what it meant that her class's math graph was going up.

> She said, "It means we are getting smarter." When she was asked, "Oh, this means you are getting smarter?" she indignantly replied, "No, it means all of us are getting smarter."

Even in a kindergarten class, quizzing students on recognition of letters (seven chosen randomly each week from 52), the students understand that a line going up means learning more and a line going down means they didn't do as well. Further, children of all ages have suggestions for improving the learning process in their classrooms.

Additional graphs available to teachers for the managing of their classroom learning are the upper and lower control limits placed over the scatter diagram (see Figure 1.4), an individual student's run chart placed

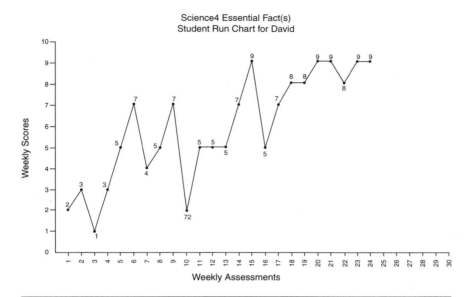

Figure 1.3 Student run chart.

over the scatter diagram (see Figure 1.5), and a histogram for specific periods of time (see Figure 1.6). The upper and lower control limits tell a teacher what her instructional system is producing and if any students are outside the system—either above or below the system.

As shown in Figure 1.6, an overlay can be provided for those instances when the parent asks, "How is my student doing compared with the rest of the class?" The overlay is a perfect answer to this question as opposed to a simple ranking answer.

Figures 1.7 and 1.8 show dramatic improvement over a period of time. This is called periodic results data.

Teachers have used quality principles to manage student learning in almost every subject from kindergarten through grade 12. In addition there are some pre-school and graduate school examples. Dr. Deming's concepts work for the learning of information (such as spelling or essential facts), performance measured with rubrics (that is, writing), performance measured by counting (that is, reading fluency, sit-ups), enthusiasm (measured on a 1–5 scale), and monitoring (that is, attendance, discipline).

Beyond the teacher and students, another powerful set of teams is grade-level teachers, department teachers, or principals and their teachers.

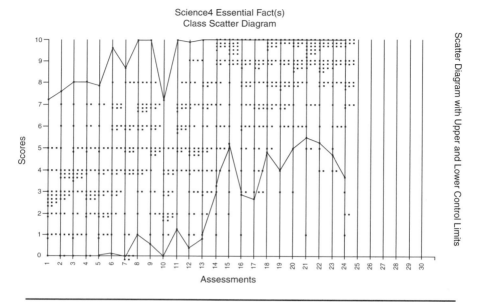

Figure 1.4 Scatter diagram with upper control limit and lower control limit.

On a regular basis these educators need time to study data for their grade level or department.

Educators in the Enterprise District (Redding, CA) collect data three times per year and make instructional decisions. Rather than have only results data in July, they have periodic results in November and February. On two full days each year they refine, share, and work for common improvements. In many locations the meetings are much more frequent. The teachers are working together to improve the whole school rather than working for the highest ranking.

LESSONS LEARNED

How data are used in managing teachers and staff is a crucial issue for American schools. School administrators, supervisors, and teachers don't treat each other well by the wide use of the "carrot and the stick." When people are having the carrot and stick applied to them, they become concerned about what kind of animal is between the carrot and the stick and know what the boss thinks of them.

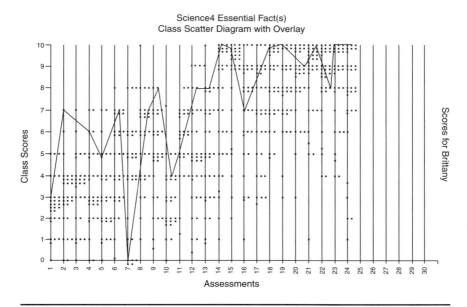

Figure 1.5 Scatter diagram with Mary's student run chart placed over the scatter diagram. Answers the question, "How is Mary doing compared to the rest of class?"

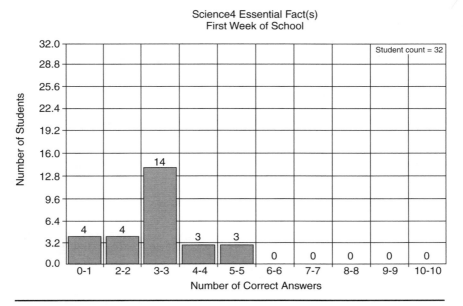

Figure 1.6 Histogram for first week of school.

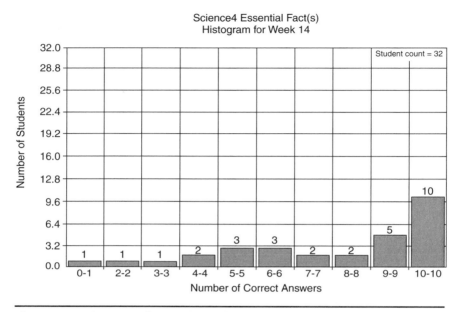

Figure 1.7 Histogram for week 14 of school year.

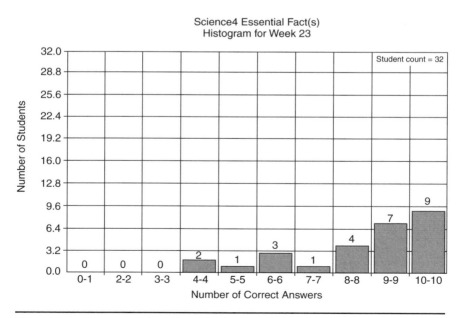

Figure 1.8 Histogram for week 23 of school year.

There is another approach to managing people that is well known to the readers of this chapter. Quality management has a long history of providing a superior manner of managing for long-term improvement. Many industries and service agencies have successfully applied quality leadership principles in their organizations.

Since 1990, some educators have looked at the teachings of Dr. W. Edwards Deming as a method of managing education. Introductions of quality have occurred at district levels for many management procedures and at school levels through Koalaty Kid™. For the most part, however, education manages its children with the same promise of reward and threat of punishment used by many in businesses. The irony is that while school administrators and teachers hate having this management approach used upon them, they apply these methods to those whom they manage.

Leaders of classrooms, schools, school districts, and other agencies have three assets: power, personality, and knowledge. All three are useful. Teachers know that if they never use power to manage a group of students, chaos results. They also know, however, that if power is the constant, then students undermine the authority of the teacher. Personality is often what people are describing when they talk about wonderful teachers. Certainly our positive personality traits help with the management of others.

This chapter is about helping teachers use knowledge as the number one management tool for the improvement of learning. Personality and power can take a back seat to knowledge. This chapter is not about knowledge of subject matter, but knowledge of students' learning. When power is the number one tool of leaders, the carrot and stick come to the forefront. So, a teacher who chooses to manage learning with knowledge can set aside the carrot and stick handed down by prior generations of leaders. What now?

A sequence of thought necessary to transition from power to knowledge follows:

1. The data that are provided to teachers in July about their students' prior year's learning are of limited value in managing learning. Applying quality tools and graphs to the data would increase their value, but the charts as presently provided to teachers are of little help.
2. Both teachers and students need accurate ongoing information about their learning every week or month throughout the school year.
3. The current sequence of studying a chapter, cramming, testing, and forgetting, does not provide teachers with the necessary knowledge to manage classroom learning.

4. If students and teachers really do know what learning is occurring in "real time," they will make the necessary adjustments to classroom procedures so that all, or almost all, of the students master the content.

The "carrot and stick" can be replaced by classroom graphs and an improved understanding of the leadership role of the teacher.

American society will not easily drop the use of fear, bribery, blame, or mandated programs in favor of quality principles. There is no hope for change if people are not even aware of a fifth possibility for managing the improvement of student learning. ASQ and other similarly minded organizations are able to make known the power of data to inform decision making and teamwork.

ABOUT THE AUTHOR

Lee Jenkins works full-time as a consultant and author in the field of quality management in education. He completed 30 years in the California public schools, 14 as a school district superintendent. In addition, Dr. Jenkins spent five years as a professor and department chair at Oregon State University. Lee and his wife, Sandy, share the joy of two married sons, two daughters-in law, and six grandchildren.

RESOURCES

Quality Press has available the following six resources that support this chapter:

Improving Student Learning: Applying Deming's Quality Principles in the Classroom by Lee Jenkins
Continuous Improvement in the Science Classroom by Jeffrey J. Burgard
Continuous Improvement in the Primary Classroom: Language Arts by Karen R. Fauss
Continuous Improvement in the History and Social Science Classroom by Shelly C. Carson
Continuous Improvement in the Mathematics Classroom by Carolyn Ayres
Class Action™ software

2

Process

Suzanne Keely

INTRODUCTION

A child taking responsibility for his or her own learning process is powerful. The school can help students take this responsibility by giving them the tools to control their own learning process. When these processes are supported by all the school's services, the prospect of lasting improvement in schools becomes a reality. This in turn prepares students for additional education, work, and community life.

For the past decade, the American Society for Quality (ASQ) has supported an initiative called ASQ Koalaty Kid. It is an educator-led continuous improvement approach bringing quality professionals together with their local schools. The approach is simple and effective, integrating theory, process, and tools. Teachers and administrators learn to implement the process approach, other quality principles, and continuous improvement methods to teach students to improve their own learning process.

PROCESS IN ACTION

The following example of the process approach used by Koalaty Kid comes from Conshohocken Elementary School in Pennsylvania (located near Philadelphia) and is reported by the principal, Darlene G. Davis. Most students walk to the community-based school. In the fall of 1995, the school served 230 kindergarten through third grade students. The student population was 56 percent Caucasian, 41 percent African-American, and 3 percent Hispanic. Fifty-six percent of the students participate in the school's free and reduced-price breakfast and lunch programs. Parents are actively encouraged to be involved in all aspects of the school through a Parent Teacher Organization, Family Fun Nights, special events and programs, and volunteering in classrooms.

The school adopted the Koalaty Kid process approach believing that it would enable students to take responsibility for their own learning processes by giving them the tools and problem-solving techniques necessary for higher education, future work, and confidence in their personal lives. In addition, it would systematically improve school practices, promote school-home-community communications, and create partnerships with community suppliers.

The school felt fortunate to have considerable support from the district superintendent, their local ASQ section, and interested community members. One such community member was an ASQ fellow and local businessperson who played a key role in helping the school begin its Koalaty Kid journey. He worked closely with the principal to build support for the project within the school district, the local ASQ section chair, teachers, and the principal. An orientation luncheon provided the setting for discussions on practical issues, such as the feasibility and value of the required training. Because of this meeting, the local ASQ section agreed to provide both financial support and the quality professionals to assist in the training. Teachers from the school attended the national Koalaty Kid Conference in the spring of 1996 and returned with enthusiasm for the project.

Koalaty Kid training sessions were held over the course of the following year. All staff members (teachers, custodians, secretaries, aides, and specialists), district office personnel, and several parents were invited to the training sessions. Participation was voluntary. Three teams that included staff, parents, and students learned and applied the plan-do-study-act (PDSA) cycle.

SIGHT-WORD VOCABULARY IMPROVEMENT TEAM

Plan: Define the System—Assess the Current Situation—Analyze Causes

Third-grade teachers felt that many of the students did not read fluently enough to handle third-grade material. Informal reading inventory (IRI) and grade-level word test data suggested that class-reading performance improved over time, but tended not to reach expected levels of reading proficiency. Teachers believed that a large part of the problem was that students had not acquired an adequate sight-word vocabulary.

The teachers decided to use the process approach to study the current system for teaching sight words and determine a plan for assisting students in that area. The team's project statement was to improve the reading sight-word system for first- and second-grade students as measured by word tests and teachers' attitudes toward the process.

A system definition diagram was used to outline key system components and attributes. Student performance data on a Dolch sight-word list were collected and reviewed by the team. Student performance on a grade-level word test and an Informal Reading Inventory (IRI) was studied as a means for determining general, grade-level reading skills over time. Analysis of the data indicated that approximately one-third of the first- and second-grade classes were performing below grade level expectations. A teacher survey indicated that there was a lack of alignment and no established procedures for teaching sight vocabulary words. Teachers felt that a systematic instructional sight word process was needed (see Figure 2.1).

A cause-and-effect diagram provided the means for identifying possible root causes of the ineffective sight-word process (see Figure 2.2).

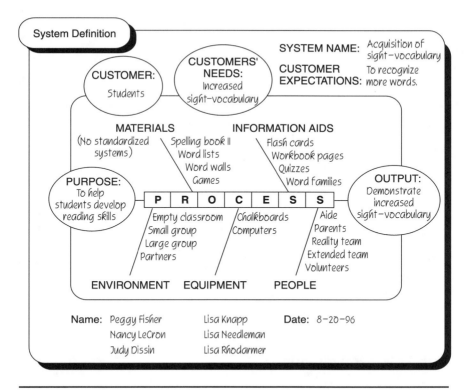

Figure 2.1 System definition diagram of sight-word vocabulary instruction.

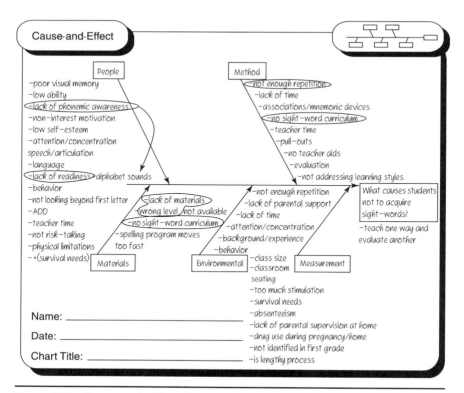

Figure 2.2 Cause-and-effect diagram on sight-word vocabulary instruction elements.

The team discussed this diagram content and selected six elements for continued study. The elements of interest were analyzed using a relations diagram in an effort to clarify the possible root causes and their effects (see Figure 2.3).

Based on results obtained from the relations diagram, the team wrote an improvement hypothesis that student fluency in reading would improve if students were given systematic, direct instruction on sight vocabulary words. An action plan provided the method for testing the hypothesis.

Do: Try Out the Method

The process improvement plan called for flexible skill grouping within the language arts teaching block on a daily basis. All first- and second-grade students would be presented with grade-level curriculum instruction as

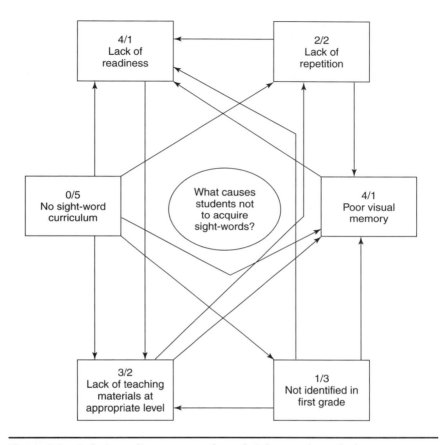

Figure 2.3 Relations diagram on selected sight-word vocabulary instruction elements.

well as 40 to 50 minutes per day of instruction based on assessed needs (for example, sight-word vocabulary).

Teachers then grouped first- and second-grade students into one of three reading process approaches based on results from three initial measures (IRI scores, sight-word reading scores, independent work skills). The three methods used were:

- Enrichment for students performing above grade level expectations
- Distributed practice for students about at grade level in terms of performance
- Highly structured for a target group of students who appeared to need systematic instruction on sight vocabulary words and other fundamental beginning reading skills

Parents were sent a letter explaining the process, the goals of the instructions, and the scheduling changes.

Study: Study the Results

After the three and one-half month trial period, the test data indicated that students had improved performance (see Figure 2.4).

The February pre-test indicated that first-grade students in the target group were able to read few of the first-grade Dolch sight-words. Words read correctly ranged from 9 to 49 words out of a possible 133 words on the list. The mean of the group was 25.33 words read correctly. Post-test data in May indicated a rise in performance. The range of correctly read first grade Dolch words was 53 to 121. The group mean was 96.87 sight-words read correctly. The target second-grade students had not mastered first-grade sight-words by February. Pre-test data of first-grade Dolch

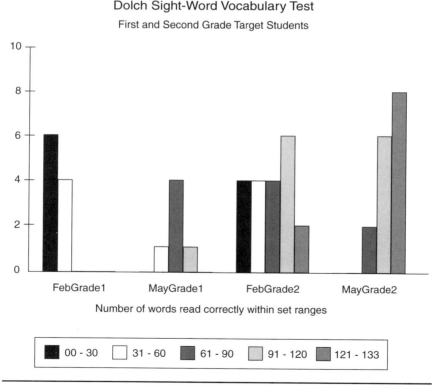

Dolch Sight-Word Vocabulary Test

First and Second Grade Target Students

Number of words read correctly within set ranges

■ 00 - 30   □ 31 - 60   ▨ 61 - 90   ▨ 91 - 120   ▨ 121 - 133

Figure 2.4 First- and second-grade target student performance on first-grade Dolch sight-words.

words read correctly were as low as 22. Two students read correctly in the 121 to 133 range. The mean score for the second-grade students was 78.31 words read correctly. Post-test data showed a range of 82 to 133 correctly read Dolch words. The group post-test mean was 116.06, suggesting that, while the students made progress, they continued to need further instruction to meet mastery level expectations.

Performance of the target first-grade students on a grade level word test in September ranged between zero to one word correct on the 20-word first grade test (mean = 0.6 words read correctly). Post-test data in May indicated a performance range of zero to nine words read correctly (mean = 3.67). Second-grade target students correctly read a pre-test range of zero to three words on the 20-word second-grade test. The post-test range was zero to 12 words read correctly. The mean number of words read correctly was 0.5 on pre-test and 4.94 words on the post-test. First- and second-grade performance on the IRI measure in September indicated that all of the target students were functioning on a reading readiness level. By May, the majority of the first-grade students were on a pre-primer level and second-grade student performance ranged up to the third grade level.

Overall, the distributions suggested a positive generalized intervention effect on the IRI measure. The team also was interested in the apparent effect of the flexible grouping strategy on the performance of all first- and second-grade students. Data suggested a general positive distribution shift in student performance on three measures (Dolch sight-word reading, grade-level word test, IRI).

Act: Standardize Improvement, Plan Continuous Improvement

Students in the first- and second-grade target groups made growth in Dolch sight-word reading and IRI performance. Performance on the grade-level word tests showed a similar pattern to that demonstrated by past classes. In terms of standardizing improvements, first- and second-grade teachers used a team approach to flexible grade level skill grouping during the 1997-98 school year. The teachers also piloted a structured reading program designed to meet the reading instruction needs of target students. The program would include a phonemic awareness component, phonetic sound out strategies, and instruction on key sight-words. The third-grade teachers agreed to try the instructional grouping strategy with the advancing second-grade students.

Lunchtime Behavior Improvement Team

The plan-do-study-act (PDSA) was also utilized to improve the lunchroom environment. The team created a system definition for the lunchtime period that outlined system purpose, components of the process, desired output, customer, and customer needs. The team developed a flowchart of the school lunch process (as shown in Figure 2.5).

The team also designed a student behavior checklist to be used in the cafeteria. Surveys were developed to assess student satisfaction with the noise level, waiting periods, general atmosphere, and whether they could hear the aides when called for lunch. Finally, a decibel meter was used to document readings on cafeteria noise levels during lunch periods. After completing a cause-and-effect diagram and studying key areas using a relations diagram, team members wrote an improvement theory that included staggered lunch times to reduce wait time. Rules were established and clearly reviewed with students. A condiment table was moved to reduce congestion in the line. Results indicated that cafeteria noise levels dropped from a mean of 78.32 decibels prior to the changes to a mean of 68.73 decibels. Behavior checklist data indicated no decrease in behavioral offenses after the changes were implemented.

The team recommended that the changes in lunch scheduling and lunch line procedures continue. They also concluded that a meeting with students to discuss further recommendations and explore ideas for increasing satisfaction with lunchtime processes was necessary for future improvements.

SPECIAL SERVICES REFERRAL IMPROVEMENT TEAM

The process approach was used to investigate the procedures and timelines involved in getting students needed assistance and to develop solutions. The team decided what areas in the referral process could be improved. After developing a system definition diagram, a flowchart of the instructional support process (IST), and a checklist for the multidisciplinary evaluation (MDE) process, the team created a cause-and-effect diagram to understand and begin to analyze possible root causes for time delays discovered by the flowchart. An improvement plan was created that eliminated steps, combined steps, and reduced the number of involved personnel in the referral processes. Root causes of the timeframe problems were reviewed and discussed with the faculty (see Table 2.1).

Table 2.1 depicts the number of days expected to complete the referral processes prior to and after changes were made in the system. The expected mean number of days stipulated for the entire process ranges from 130 to 140 days, depending on whether an additional 10 days of intervention were needed in the instructional support process. Prior to the changes, a mean number of 183 days were used to complete the process (range = 138–212). After the changes, a mean number of 127 days

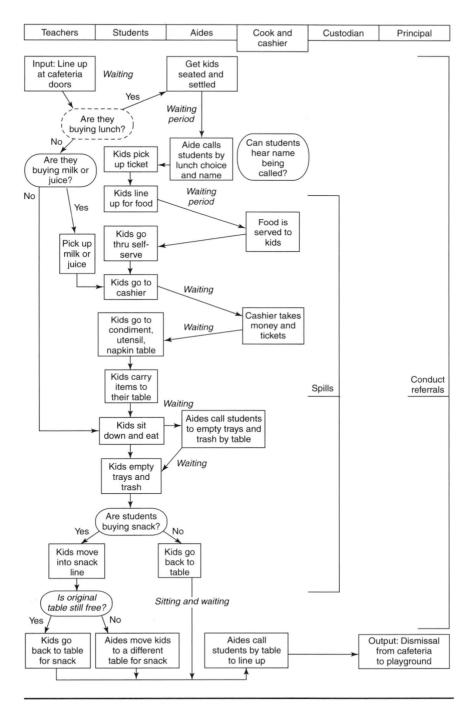

Figure 2.5 Flowchart of school lunch processes.

Table 2.1   A comparison of the expected number of days for comleting a special services referral and the number of days used to complete cases prior to and after system changes.

Data on Special Needs Referral Timeframes

Timeframes and Steps

	Student	20 days—First referral, data gathering, problem-solving meeting	30 days—Intervention and follow up meeting	10 days—Additional intervention days if needed	10 days—MDE referral process (routing of information sheet)	45 days—Data gathered, report written and received by school	5 days—Signatures on CER, CER sent to district office	10 days—District office personnel obtain parental signature. CER received by school secretary. IEP scheduled.	10 days—IEP meeting held	130 days—Total days (140 days if additional IST time needed)
Before changes	1	23	23	—	37	59	25	4	7	178
	2	17	28	—	24	103	11	19	*10	212
	3	30	27	—	66	53	14	29	9	201
	4	20	29	—	36	52	1	0	0	138
	5	22	37	—	29	71	7	4	12	182
	6	23	61	—	20	69	7	4	2	186
	Mean	23	35	0	35	68	11	10	7	183
After changes	7	18	30	—	4	57	4	1	2	123
	8	17	30	—	4	40	9	21	10	139
	9	20	28	—	1	49	6	*20	*10	134
	10	20	28	—	1	48	4	1	0	112
	Mean	19	29	0	3	49	6	11	9	127

Number of days (row label spanning the Before changes and After changes sections)

*Default number. Process ongoing or completed elsewhere.

were used to complete the process (range = 112–139), indicating significant improvement time needed.

The faculty were surveyed again to determine whether there were changes in their perceptions of the special services referral process. Despite data indicating that the amount of time needed to complete the process was within the timeframes stipulated in state guidelines, several individuals continued to be unsatisfied with the time frames.

The survey results also indicated that staff did not feel the need for further in-servicing on the basic process. In reviewing the results of the project, team members were pleased with the improvements in the amount of time used to complete steps in the overall referral process. The team decided that all major project steps should be continued and standardized. The team also recommended in-service training for new faculty and any staff members interested in reviewing the referral process information. Team members also recommended that a master check-sheet, similar to the one used in the instructional support process, be developed for the MDE process. They felt that the check-sheet would be helpful in monitoring progress on referrals over time.

Improvement Actions

At the end of the school year, members of the project teams reviewed project findings and recommendations with the entire faculty. Ongoing monitoring of improvement efforts was recommended by all of the teams in order to maintain the positive impact from the initial system changes. Consensus-based faculty decisions were made to follow through with team recommendations. Follow-through on those recommendations and decisions began at the start of the 1997 school year.

Staff members chose to emphasize school spirit as well as the substance component of the Koalaty Kid process as part of their ongoing effort to maintain positive school changes and begin implementing future continuous improvements. Plans included helping students become skilled users of quality tools and leaders in exhibiting quality behaviors as members of the school community.

LESSONS LEARNED

Koalaty Kid saw immediate improvement when the following components were present:

- The culture for continuous improvement had already been created. This is one in which leadership is shared at all levels, and teamwork is present.
- The champion for continuous improvement is the superintendent. The superintendent is active and present in the process. The process is utilized throughout the district, rather than at isolated schools.
- There is an understanding of the Baldrige in Education Criteria for Performance Excellence as a framework for improvement and a willingness to adapt it to the school district.
- Where there is not leadership from the superintendent, there is strong leadership at the school level whether it is administrators or teachers.

THE KOALATY KID APPROACH TO PROCESS

As seen in the above example, the process approach of Koalaty Kid has a comprehensive design. Because it is an approach, not a curriculum, each school tailors the general elements to its own particular needs whether that involves instruction, assessment, classroom management, or school development. Guidelines are purposely broad to encourage schools to make Koalaty Kid "their own." In addition, each school develops its own system for recognizing and celebrating its successes.

Over the past decade, the process approach has been developed and improved with feedback from K–12 educators. The Center for Total Quality Schools at Pennsylvania State University researched and validated the approach in 1997. Because of the success at the elementary and middle school levels, the concept expanded to the high school level in 1998. The high school counterpart is called Koalaty Keys. The process approach and training are the same.

Koalaty Kid and Keys utilize W. Edwards Deming's four-step data-driven Plan-Do-Study-Act cycle for process improvement. To use the cycle effectively, specific tools are taught and used in analyzing the data collected and in improving processes. Teams learn to use tools such as affinity diagrams, brainstorming, fishbone diagrams, flowcharts, Pareto diagrams, and operational definition within the PDSA cycle.

Training can be implemented in a number of ways. The model used most frequently is to identify a team of teachers, administrators, staff, parents, business partners, ASQ section members, and/or students assembled into teams of five to 30 people who have a stake in the system being studied for improvement. One or more schools may be represented on the team. The training is conducted during six full-day sessions over a four to eight month period. The first two days are consecutive, with approximately a month between each of the last four days. This can be flexible and is determined between the team and the trainer. The participants work on an actual project they choose during the first two days, and receive facilitation and feedback, as well as instruction on the process from their trainer. Two or more participants from that team then do a weeklong training that prepares them to be on-site "experts" in disseminating and coordinating Koalaty Kid throughout their school or district. In many cases, ASQ section members continue to mentor the schools even after they have finished initial training.

THE KOALATY KID PROCESS WORKS

Repeatedly, ASQ hears about the remarkable improvements occurring in Koalaty Kid-trained schools. Many teams, having learned the power of the tools, identify projects to work on that affect not just their classrooms, but their schools and districts as well. Schools implementing this approach often find immediate improvement in the area chosen as a project.

For long-term impact, with integration into all of the systems of the school, implementation and sustained improvement often takes several years to be firmly established. Sustaining continuous improvement in education is dependent on leadership, just as it is in other industries. One of the greatest barriers to success is administrators leaving key positions, or new administrators not understanding the process and putting it aside. If the systems have not yet taken a firm hold in the culture of the school or district, this can effectively halt progress. For this reason, having support from a business partner and ASQ Section can help educators prevail in the process, as does including the superintendent and principals in training and using the process.

RESULTS FROM USING THE PROCESS APPROACH

The following schools learned how to define their processes, collect their data, and use the resulting information effectively to make data-driven decisions that drive improvement in the classrooms and schools. In each of the following examples, the schools involved had principals, and in some cases superintendents, that participated in training, problem solving, and facilitating the identified improvements. In all situations, the schools addressed issues of real concern to the stakeholders and improved the processes to attain their goals.

Mark Twain Elementary School in Richardson, TX, was historically the lowest performing, poorest school in the district. Dallas area property values are tied to the district's standardized test results. Principal David Sanders introduced the idea of utilizing quality tools and processes to drive improvement. They needed to improve, regardless of being one of the poorest schools in the district, and they did. They utilized the PDSA cycle as their approach to improving the student-learning environment, clearly defined expectations and recognition, and focused on improving academics. After one year, their results on the Texas Assessment of Academic Skills (TAAS) for schoolwide achievement showed the greatest gain in the district. Writing/comprehension pass rates increased from 72 percent to 93 percent. Mathematics pass rates increased from 65 percent to 81 percent. Over the course of three years, the overall rate of passing rose from 35 percent to 71 percent.

Horace Mann Elementary School in Shawnee, OK, is a Title 1 school: 98 percent free/reduced-price lunch. Before Koalaty Kid training occurred, the third graders were identified as being "at-risk." Under the leadership of principal Leota Youngblood, the school began by addressing student behavior and attitude first; academic achievement followed. After one year of implementation, behavior and attitude that affect the learning environment improved. Bus misconduct incidents decreased from 112 to 33. Disrespect—for example, talking back, refusing to do work-incidents decreased from 674 to 38. When Koalaty Kid was used to address academic achievement, the results from the Iowa Test of Basic Skills improved after one year. Third graders gained 26 points in Reading, 23 points in Language Arts, 24 points in Math, and 20 points in Composition.

In Avon School in Grayslake, IL, principal Pam Cullotta utilized the systematic approach to focus on improving their IGAP Standardized Test Results from 1995 to 1997: Reading pass rates improved from 13 percent to 33 percent. Math pass rates improved from 14 percent to 44 percent. Writing pass rates improved from 24 percent to 32 percent. In addition, the following achievements were realized:

California Achievement Test Scores (percentage of students scoring average or above)

	Language	Math	Science	Social Studies
3rd Grade	91%	96%	100%	96%
4th Grade	93%	100%	94%	94%
5th Grade	95%	96%	95%	100%

Junction Elementary School in Kansas City, KS, is an urban neighborhood school setting and one of five elementary schools in the Turner School District. The school faces challenges common to many urban districts. Among its 400 students, almost 50 percent are eligible for free or reduced-price lunches. In addition, 60 percent of its kindergarten students are considered at-risk.

In 1996, Turner District Superintendent Winona Winn decided to explore Koalaty Kid as one means of helping Junction Elementary address problems associated with chronic underachievement in meeting the Kansas and North Central Accreditation requirements. According to the principal, Allan Amos, they were in a panic state. Expectations for improvement were clear, and earning the accreditation was essential. They desperately needed a system that could help them address the goals and establish a focus needed to achieve them.

Through their involvement with ASQ Koalaty Kid, the staff created an environment for continuous improvement, recognizing rising test scores and individual students' grade improvement, and an ever-improving safe and orderly learning climate. Initially introduced to help the school improve on a disappointing record of achievement in Kansas and North Central

Accreditation tests, the process also had an impressive effect on student behavior.

Improvements and achievements since implementing ASQ Koalaty Kid training in 1996 include:

- A reduction from 13.9 percent to 4 percent of fourth-grade students scoring unsatisfactory on the Kansas Math Assessment Test
- Twenty-percentile improvement in Iowa Test of Basic Skills scores over a five-year period in fifth-grade reading and math
- 96 percent of fourth-grade students scoring above or at basic level on the Kansas Math Assessment Test
- 99 percent of fifth graders scoring above or at basic level on the Kansas Writing Assessment Test
- 91 percent of fifth graders above or at basic level on the Kansas Reading Assessment Test
- A 50 percent reduction in discipline office referrals over a three-year period
- Data-driven instructional decisions
- Meeting all Kansas and North Central Accreditation requirements
- Reading, writing, and math assessment scores that exceed both the district and state averages
- State recognition with the 2000 Kansas Award for Excellence, Level II

Ridgeview Elementary School in Ashtabula, OH, piloted the original Koalaty Kid training process. The Ashtabula Section 812 of the American Society for Quality (ASQ) [formerly the American Society for Quality Control] and Key-Bank (formerly Society Bank) were partners in the training and implementation of the Koalaty Kid approach at Ridgeview.

Mary Jo Taylor, principal at Ridgeview Elementary, said, "The Koalaty Kid approach is really a process for making improvements. We are: number one, committed to improvement; number two, committed to collecting and using data; and number three, committed to teamwork. Everyone is responsible. Everyone has a say."

Because of this commitment and to help provide the mechanism for input into school operations, seven teams emerged to handle different aspects of the school's operations. The strategic quality planning team is responsible for providing direction, managing the entire process, and overseeing the other six teams. The other six teams are the staff development team, technology team, proficiency team, parental involvement team, intervention team, and lunch time/discipline team.

The Ohio State Department of Education requires all schools and school districts in the State of Ohio to write a continuous improvement plan. The following definition of continuous improvement was taken from the Department of Education's Web site. "Continuous Improvement: In Ohio, a continuous improvement plan is a document used to guide educators, students and their families, business people, and community members in the process of achieving and measuring substantial improvements in the school district's performance." Since Ridgeview Elementary had been planning annual improvements utilizing the Koalaty Kid process, it became a relatively easy transition to meet the requirements for the continuous improvement plan required by the Department of Education.

Since 1994 and the implementation of this process, improvement has been made in the following areas:

- The number of discipline referrals dropped from a high of 220 in the 1992–93 school year to 130 in the 2000–01 school year.
- The number of parent volunteers increased from 27 in 1998 to 76 in 2001.
- The number of families participating in the Ridgeview Family Reading Program increased from 39 percent in 1997 to 57 percent in 2001.
- The number of teachers participating in peer coaching increased from 13 in 1999 to 23 in 2000.
- The level of teaching became more sophisticated. Teachers now share best practices and have worked to achieve alignment in curriculum. Learning goals, common teaching structures, and assessments are coordinated across the grades.

Test scores improved dramatically as well from 1996 to 2001:

- In fourth grade, writing test results improved by 46.4 points: from 30.6 to 77
- In sixth grade, writing tests results jumped 36.9 points: from 43.1 to 80
- Sixth grade reading test results increased 33.5 points: from 34.5 to 68

The Growth Partnership in Ashtabula County presented the Best of the County award to the school in 1998. Success of the program and its impact on students, faculty, and parents merited Ridgeview one of Ohio's five state quality awards in 2001. They also earned the Ohio Award for Excellence at Level 1 in 2001.

Community Consolidated School District #15 is a K–8 school district led by Superintendent John Conyers. It is the second largest K–8 district in Illinois and the first to implement the Koalaty Kid methodology district-wide. Implemented throughout its 19 schools, the Plan-Do-Study-Act (PDSA) process is used to focus their goals on the district Student Performance Targets that are determined by the School Board and its constituents. Each school sets its own specific measurable goals along with a timetable for charting the progress. The improvement teams within each school provide leadership that keep it focused on targeted district goals. Measured results include:

- Teacher satisfaction at one school improving from 54 percent to 84 percent in four years
- Third grade math scores at one school increasing from 84 percent meeting or exceeding to 97 percent in one year
- Fifth grade reading scores increasing in two schools: from 83 percent meeting or exceeding to 93 percent in one year at one, and from 76 percent meeting or exceeding to 90 percent in one year at another

Pekin Public Schools District 108, in Illinois, led by Superintendent Perry Soldwedl, began to create the culture for their quality journey four years ago. The K–12 district aligned their curriculum with state standards in the areas of reading, writing, and math from pre-kindergarten through eighth grade. Along with alignment, rubrics for learning expectations in those areas were created. Focusing on the fundamentals of these core areas became an expectation for teachers, students, and parents.

In year two, they developed districtwide assessments in the same areas of reading, writing, and math. They focused on data and feedback to guide teaching and learning. In year three, after searching for ways to drive the improvement down into the classroom, the superintendent implemented districtwide training to support the development of better instructional practices in reading, writing, and math.

During the 2000-01 school year, the district began utilizing the Koalaty Kid PDSA process and tools with five of their 10 schools. Each of the schools formed a team that focused on one improvement theory. This resulted in one school designing and implementing a schoolwide management program for students. The results of this program were:

- Reduced absenteeism
- Lower disciplinary referrals
- Increased homework completion

Another school focused on low writing test results in the Illinois Standard Achievement Test. They focused their efforts on three areas of the writing rubric and developed suggestions for teaching and learning. The school increased the number of students who exceeded or met writing standards by 27 percent in one year.

By the end of the 2000–01 school year, 25 percent of the teachers had participated in training and enthusiasm had spread, creating a support system that flourished. Those going through the initial training were further trained to be facilitators and mentors to the rest of the district. During the 2001–02 school year, the district conducted more training and provided support for all 10 schools to develop an action plan to address student achievement through the PDSA improvement process. The teams meet periodically throughout the year to share data collection tools, strategies, improvement theories, and progress. The district Web site posts data collection systems that collect data around the seven Baldrige criteria.

CONCLUSION

The Process Approach

As seen in these examples from schools, the process approach facilitates a school's ability to identify students' learning processes, to understand support services, and to optimize their interdependencies. It also enables students to define and control their own learning processes. They learn to transform facts and data into useful information. They learn to use the resources provided and to regulate their own performance variability.

The schools learn that processes can be combined so teachers and staff members collectively can achieve a planned purpose. The results from one process can be an input to another process and can be combined in a process chain. Student responsibilities, school procedures, and district resources can be effectively established, efficiently maintained, and continually improved.

The interdependencies of a school systems' activities are often more complex than those found in business and industry. This chapter highlights the main value of a process approach and helps schools to understand how each process influences the student's ability to meet curriculum requirements. Koalaty Kid emphasizes the need to clarify interfaces, responsibilities, and authorities, as well as to facilitate continual improvement.

This requires determining the:

- School's quality policy and objectives
- Learning processes critical to attaining objectives
- Effect each process has on learning objectives
- Root causes for ineffective processes
- Priority of process improvements to provide optimum results

The Koalaty Kid process approach can be applied to maintaining, developing, and improving an existing quality management system. By implementing an adequate quality management system, an organization creates confidence in the capability and reliability of its processes as well as the basis for continual improvement. Both lead to student success, stakeholder satisfaction, and confidence in the school as a continuing asset for the community.

ABOUT THE AUTHOR

Suzanne Keely taught for almost a decade. Working at the American Society for Quality (ASQ) since 1993, she learned about implementing quality in the workplace. As Koalaty Kid manager for ASQ, she has been working with educators in their quality journeys for the past two years.

3

Leadership in Reading Improvement

Judyth Zaczkowski and E. Kenneth Buckley

INTRODUCTION

This chapter describes the leadership shown by two principals and 19 third- and fourth-grade teachers in Lake County, OH, using Deming's Plan-Do-Study-Act problem-solving cycle. Its purpose was to implement leadership based upon Deming's beliefs to design a "Profile for Reading Success."

There is no disagreement that teaching children to read has profound implications for what we have come to value—differing ideas freely expressed, debated, and openly discussed in a local marketplace that can now be defined as a world wide web. Yet, as a new century begins, there appears to be more and more children who are not becoming proficient readers.

The problem is not that educators have suddenly forgotten how to teach children to read. The problem is that children of today need to read far better than their parents. The at-risk readers of 1960 could find worthwhile employment because 60 percent of the jobs required unskilled labor. In the beginning of this new century, however, it is estimated that only 15 percent of the jobs will require unskilled workers.

According to *WORKPLACE BASICS: The Skills Employers Want*, students who had difficulty in school are included in the following bleak percentages:

68 percent were arrested

85 percent became unwed mothers

79 percent were welfare dependents

85 percent were dropouts

72 percent were unemployed

Since the ability to read is the prerequisite skill for academic success, the overwhelming majority of the actual faces comprising these grim statistics were once children who did not learn to read at a proficient level.

LEADERSHIP

Some state legislators seek to solve this problem by enacting into law high stakes end-of-the-year tests. This is true in the State of Ohio because the legislature has set a 75 percent passing rate on the grade four reading proficiency test and enacted the Fourth Grade Guarantee, which recommends that fourth-grade students not passing the test be retained.

While data pertaining to student reading achievement are certainly necessary, the tracking of progress by looking at only end-of-the-year results in order to improve reading achievement ignores the need for identifying and using systematic data during the instructional process to make effective midcourse adjustments.

Unfortunately, when the generally unsatisfactory results are released to the community and the public criticism begins, too many educational leaders respond by hunkering down in their self-constructed bunkers to defend themselves against these slings and arrows. While occupying a bunker may appear to be a successful strategy for survival, the French and the Germans learned during World War II, as did many armies that came before them, that building bunkers too often provides nothing more than a false sense of security. Further, since bunkers are built to take a defensive posture (never an offensive one), it is impossible to provide truly effective leadership from inside a bunker.

Educational leaders have something in common with generals, for they too must lead an army. Of course, there is a critical difference when it comes to the purpose of an educational army. An army of teachers must provide the necessary tools to its students so that they can enter the adult world with the power to enlighten the future.

In the field of reading, a lack of an adequate research base to guide reading instruction to equip children with these necessary tools is not a major issue. In the past three decades, there has been an explosion of knowledge in that arena.

Rather, leadership is needed to manage processes for implementing research findings in a deliberate, systematic manner by gathering and analyzing significant data to determine what works and what does not, and this requires a new perspective about educational leadership.

As W. Edwards Deming once said, "We can do something about our problems or continue the way we are." In other words, we can stay in the bunker or climb out to seriously study the view.

The core of Deming's philosophy is embodied in his Fourteen Points. Institute leadership is point number seven. Deming believed the following about a leader's role:

A leader's job is to help his people.

A leader is a coach not a judge; judging people does not help them.

A leader must have knowledge.

A leader must be able to teach.

A leader must also determine, by objective methods, which employees are in need of help.

LEADERSHIP IN READING

How to really help teachers improve the reading achievement of their students became the vital question. Gaining knowledge became the new quest because compiling the data from the end-of-the-year results was not providing the knowledge teachers and administrators required for true improvement in reading achievement. Formative indicators of reading achievement were designed and then administered throughout the year to 173 grade three students and 172 grade four students to develop an effective information and analysis system. The results of these indicators were then statistically screened and weighted by the results of the year-end summative reading measure to identify formative benchmarks to be used in the following two ways: (1) to identify those students who were at risk of failing the year-end reading test; and (2) to provide teachers with significant data to determine the effectiveness of their in-process reading instructional strategies.

In this respect, this project is different than the more typical ones where specific reading instructional techniques are utilized and studied to determine if they were effective. We believed that first there must be an information and analysis system based upon the needs of the stakeholders in place before various techniques should be tried. Without such a system, it is impossible to determine what techniques are truly required, and if they will meet the needs of the stakeholders; and, without such a system, it is impossible to provide leadership, because without such a system it is impossible to gain knowledge.

Designing the System: Plan

Ohio was one of the six states selected to disseminate the *Baldrige Educational Criteria for Performance Excellence* to the state's public K–12 schools as a framework to guide performance. The Baldrige framework is based upon research derived from high-performing organizations. There are seven criteria, which are based upon 11 interrelated core values and concepts.

While all of the values are interrelated, the Core Values inherent within this project included Visionary Leadership; Learning-Centered Education; Valuing Faculty, Staff, and Partners; Agility; and Management by Fact.

Management by Fact requires many types of data and information to determine, among other things, projections of future performance. Since the only available reading data came from the end-of-the-year test results from the state's proficiency tests, the reams of reports received in June contained much information but no real knowledge. According to Deming, information is about the past; knowledge is about predicting the future because, as he said, "Managing by results is like driving while looking in the rear view mirror." All a driver can see is what is behind him, and this does nothing to guide him to his destination.

Since no formative indicators existed to measure reading process improvement, neither principals nor teachers could judge whether students were improving and, therefore, had no way to determine which instructional practices were effective or ineffective. These year-end achievement test scores were clearly insufficient for the practical purpose of improving the ongoing reading process and providing the Visionary Leadership required to ensure that systems, strategies, and methods for achieving excellence were in place.

One reason schools lacked systematic formative data was because of a deeply rooted teacher-centered environment where teacher behavior was measured for annual evaluations rather than results reflected in improved student learning performance. This was in sharp contrast to a Learning-Centered Education, a Baldrige core value, which relies upon results based upon standards—the measurement process characteristics—and formative (in process) measures of achievement.

Within the Baldrige framework's description of a Learning-Centered Education, the authors write, "Formative assessment is used to measure learning early in the learning process and to tailor learning experiences to individual needs and learning styles."

The use of formative data, which focuses on the progress of the group as well as that of individual students, is critical in improving the reading process. Yet, this type of testing and measurement often creates anxiety in teachers. This is inconsistent with Deming's quality philosophy "Drive out fear" from the workplace. The assumption is that employees must feel secure before they begin to generate ideas to improve productivity and services.

The employees who do the job have the best ideas about improvements that are needed. Teachers are the frontline workers in the classrooms. Cunningham and Allington have written in *Classrooms That Work: They Can All Read and Write,* "Classroom teachers are the most important factor in the success or failure of at-risk children in our schools."

Further, Deming points out the need "to remove barriers to pride of workmanship." He found there were very few employees who did not want to do a good job. It was the system's problems, such as a lack of good materials, sound training, and proper equipment, that most often stood in the way.

Experienced K–12 administrators work with teachers who take pride in their instructional expertise and spend much time and energy constructing plans they hope will ensure increased student learning. However, they need guidance in both understanding system requirements and that the gathering and analyzing of data is critical to fulfill these requirements. Clearly, teacher attitudes about systematic data needed to change if improvements were to be ongoing.

Inherent within the core value of Valuing Faculty, Staff, and Partners is the concept that "an organization's success depends increasingly on the knowledge, skills, innovative creativity, and motivation of its faculty, staff, and partners." This means making a commitment to their development as well as their well being.

Helping teachers understand that data are neutral and, as Tom Casperson, Director of the Ohio Award of Excellence, has said, "Facts are friendly things," coincided with a pivotal desire to identify a series of formative indicators of reading achievement, measured throughout the year, that could be used in two main ways:

- To track reading improvement of the group and individuals to help teachers assess how the class is doing at specific intervals of the year to provide quickly specific reading interventions where needed, or to change instructional practices for the group.
- To collect data from the indicators and, through a statistical screening process to establish a profile that would create benchmarks to predict reading success on the fourth-grade reading proficiency test. In this way, teachers and parents would know, at different points in the year, which students were in need of help.

This also touches upon the core value of Agility. Effective organizations develop the capacity for not only incorporating more flexibility into their processes but also for increasing the rapidity of responses to problems. Using only end-of-the-year results leaves a teacher with only his/her intuitive guesses as to why individual children did not pass, and the following year's teacher is left playing the game of catch-up.

It was, therefore, necessary to move beyond managing by results. In order to do this, data were needed to help school leaders gain knowledge to be able to predict and, consequently, to help teachers gain knowledge about the students in their rooms. They then use this knowledge to monitor the growth of the entire group, as well as individual students. This type of data would eventually lead to making knowledgeable instructional changes and to designing knowledgeable, individual interventions.

Since there is no one indicator to measure reading achievement, effective multiple indicators had to be found. The data gathered from these indicators would then be used to develop a profile for reading success at the end of the school year to be utilized during subsequent years as formative benchmarks for students in grades three and four. These indicators would act as variables and be subsequently weighted by the year-end passing score on the summative evaluation. In this way, knowledge would be gained to enable teachers and administrators to begin making predictions about a child's reading instructional needs to achieve reading success. After considerable research and study, four indicators were selected.

This ended the first phase of the problem-solving task in Deming's PDSA cycle.

Designing the System: DO

Nineteen third- and fourth-grade teachers from three different school districts in Lake County, OH—Mentor, Madison, and Willoughby-Eastlake—volunteered for this project. Third- and fourth-grade teachers were selected because of the state's focus on grade four, and in terms of management and securing volunteers. Two grade levels would ease management of the data and require the recruiting of fewer volunteers than if all the grade levels were studied.

Eight of the volunteers came from two schools, and the rest were secured from the *Summer Intervention of Reading Instruction* course taught in 2000. Since this particular session was designed for teachers in grades three and four, it was not difficult to find volunteers once the project was explained.

Since providing the proper resources is also a quality of good leadership, a grant for approximately $9000 was written that was then funded by the Martha Holden Jennings Foundation. The funding provided for such expenses as secretarial assistance to enter the data; $250 per teacher to spend on reading instructional materials; the purchase of testing materials; and obtaining food for meetings.

The criteria used to identify effective multiple indicators for reading were based upon the following:

- Research in reading. All indicators at these grade levels should measure comprehension of reading materials. Without comprehension, there is no reading, even if a student could pronounce the words correctly.
- A correlation to the year-end summative evaluation of 0.5 or above.
- The ability of districts to replicate these indicators in their schools.
- The ability of these measures to assist teachers to gain knowledge about student achievement at multiple times throughout the year.
- The ease with which teachers could administer the indicators.

The first indicator selected was The Gates-MacGinitie Reading Survey test. This was to be the standardized instrument. This test had been administered at Sterling Morton Elementary School for the four previous years to students in grades K–4. At that time, the district had no summative evaluation for students in the primary grades. While the subjects of this research became only students in grades 3–4, Sterling Morton had continued to utilize this test after the district adopted off-year proficiency tests for students in grades 1–3. A correlation of 0.7 or higher with the Gates-MacGinitie test was found at all grade levels.

The Gates test also gives results in Normal Curve Equivalents (NCEs). These are scores that have been scaled to always reflect a mean of 50 and a standard deviation of 21.06 in the normative sample for a given test. NCEs always range from 1 to 99 and may appear similar to percentiles, but their advantage is that, unlike percentiles, they are based on an equal interval scale. This makes the data they provide much easier to manipulate statistically.

The test was administered in October to give teachers information about the reading abilities of their class at the beginning of the year. This was the only indicator in our profile that was administered only once. Once the profile was designed, the results of this standardized measure could be used to identify those students who might be in need, as well as determine if the majority of the class was at-risk.

Dr. Mark Shinn's research, along with others, had indicated a correlation between reading comprehension and reading fluency. This is the rate at which students read. Proficient readers read not word by word but with proper phrasing of the text. They have developed another important reading concept called *automaticity*. Quite simply, they know the words when they see them. Every time a child must stop in the middle of a passage to figure out one or more unknown words, comprehension of that passage is interrupted and meaning is lost.

Dr. Shinn developed curriculum-based measurement reading fluency probes to test a student's fluency rate. To use a medical analogy, these probes are similar to taking a child's temperature. If the thermometer registers a temperature above 98.6, there is a problem. This does not give the doctor enough knowledge to make a diagnosis. It is only an indicator of a problem. The same is true with the reading fluency probes.

Three probes are administered, and students have one minute to reach each one. The number of words read correctly on each probe is tallied, and the median score is selected as the child's fluency rate. The purpose of selecting the median score is to monitor what has been called "The Russian Novel Syndrome." Any child, even a proficient reader, may encounter problems on a selected probe. Administering three probes and taking the median score allows a teacher to gain more accurate information about a child's fluency rate.

Further, these probes may be administered as often as necessary throughout the year. For example, if a teacher is testing a specific reading intervention with a student, the teacher may give these probes on a weekly basis to monitor improvement.

A curriculum-based measurement probe is generally administered from the actual reading text. However, a standard set were also developed. Since data were being gathered from three school districts, all of which utilized different texts, a uniform measurement was needed. Further, since the accuracy of the profile would depend upon the probes the students were reading, it was important that all students read from the same third- or fourth-grade probes. These probes were designated as, simply, reading fluency probes.

Shinn's work also utilized the administration of a Maze test, which is a reading activity where a child reads a passage with every nth word deleted. Usually three choices are given for the missing word, and the child must select the one that makes the most sense within the passage. These tests and their counterpart, a Cloze passage, have long been used as a quick test to determine comprehension levels.

The STAR reading test, published by Reading Renaissance, was selected as the main Maze instrument. This publisher also produces the Accelerated Reader Program that was available to 14 of the 19 teachers. This particular Maze test had several advantages. It could be administered five times during the school year. Next, it is both a norm-referenced and criterion-based test. Among the results it generated were scores given in NCEs. Since the test is administered on the computer, the software had the ability to restructure the test continually, based upon the students' previous responses, and both students and teachers were provided with instant feedback as soon as they could press the "print" button. Finally, the results also provided an instructional reading level.

Everyone, children and adults, have three basic reading levels: independent, instructional, and frustration. When people read text and need no help to interpret it, that is the independent level. The instructional level is that point where people need help to master the text; but, crucially, it can be mastered with instruction. At the frustration level, the reader shuts down and, even with instruction, cannot meaningfully understand the text.

All readers improve their reading achievement at the instructional level. Lev Vygotsky, a Russian psychologist, formulated his "Zone of Proximal Development" as the area where the learner is challenged and, therefore, learning can occur. Drawing an analogy from *The Three Bears*, it is not "too hot" and it is "not too cold;" it is "just right." If the reading is too easy, no learning will occur; and if it is too difficult, no learning will occur. The STAR test attempted to identify the learner's "Zone of Proximal Development."

Since variation is a fact of life, a classroom full of children often has a wide variation among reading abilities. Giving children textual material that is too difficult does not make them better readers. Deming said, "When people try to do what they cannot do, they wish to give up." The same is true with children. Richard Allington, at a Teaching and Learning Conference in Columbus, OH, in 2000, remarked how the typical at-risk readers generally spend every school day interacting with text they cannot read.

Learning to read is a skill that must be practiced in much the same way that a musical instrument is mastered. However, a pivotal study conducted by Deloris Durkin in 1979 demonstrated that the average fourth-grade student read approximately four minutes per day. Students completed worksheets, and were given time to read stories, but sustained reading—the kind that is needed for improvement—in books at their reading level approximated the time given above.

The Accelerated Reader Program is designed to have students reading books at their individual levels for sustained periods of time. Since 14 of the 19 teachers had access to this program, the final indicator would be the grade equivalent score.

The five teachers not having access to this program still wanted to participate, and we did not want to exclude anyone. Therefore, a Maze test was constructed for these teachers. However, all students did take this Maze test during the year.

One hundred and seventy-three third-grade students and 172 fourth-grade students participated in this study. All students were assigned numbers to preserve confidentiality.

With two exceptions, all indicators were administered at three points during the year: September, January, and May. Teachers were coached in the administration of all indicators. However, since part of the plan was to help teachers realize that data were nothing to fear, the data were not collected and then dropped into a statistical black hole until the end of the year when the actual profiles were developed.

Teachers received reports in the form of histograms after the indicators were administered and the teachers were trained in interpreting them. The histograms monitored the third- and fourth-grade groups as a whole, as well as the upper, middle, and lower quartiles, to ensure that there was equity in the process. Each teacher also received the same reports for his/her individual group. Means, medians, standard deviations, and the progress made in each quartile were monitored. Further, these histograms also identified outliers in each group both as a whole and in each individual teacher's classroom.

Once the data were entered, a trusty software program provided these graphs and the accompanying data with just the click of the mouse. Not once were calculators used or points plotted on graph paper. Basic descriptive statistics are important tools for studying processes. A leader does *not* have to be a statistician, but he/she does have to have basic knowledge of statistics. There are many software programs on the market to calculate the mean and standard deviation of group data and to create graphs to help understand the results. (See Figure 3.1.)

The first set of graphs provided the baseline data. The second and third sets were the most important for the purpose of demonstrating to teachers that data were not to be feared. The hypothesis was that for the first time, these teachers would be seeing objective, formative data that did indicate students in their classrooms were making progress, rather than waiting until the end of the year to discover who had passed or failed the proficiency test and wondering what it was that they could have done better. Further, once teachers realized that students were making some progress through their instructional efforts, they would be more willing to evaluate opportunities for improvement objectively.

The definition for continuous improvement was if the mean had increased and the standard deviation had decreased. This was because the mean could increase because a few students had dramatically improved, but if the standard deviation increased then the entire group was not progressing. T-tests of the means were also performed to discover if there were significant differences between the various means.

The results confirmed our hypothesis. Students were making progress and improving their reading achievement in all quartiles. Meetings with teachers demonstrated their interest in the data they were receiving. They were beginning to use the data to inform their practice.

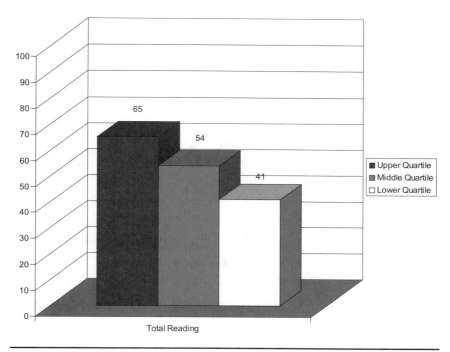

Figure 3.1   Grade three: The upper, middle, and lower quartile results of the total reading score from the Gates-MacGinitie reading survey test administered in fall 2000.

Designing the System: STUDY

The first significant data received were the results of the Gates-MacGinitie reading test. The Gates test gives scores for vocabulary, comprehension, and a total reading score, which is a composite of the two tests. Figure 3.1 depicts the results from the total reading score given in NCEs for the total third-grade group.

A score of 50 NCEs is considered average. A student who earned that score was reading approximately at grade level. The median score was 54 with a mean of 54.22. However, a Means Anova t-test utilizing the Tukey-Kramer method revealed that four of the 10 classroom means were significantly lower, with means of 43.76, 45.5, 43.67, and 47.47. This meant that these teachers were starting their year with a group of children who had more serious reading needs than the others.

Figure 3.2 represents the total reading score from fourth grade. The results from the fourth grade depicted a median of 56 with a mean of

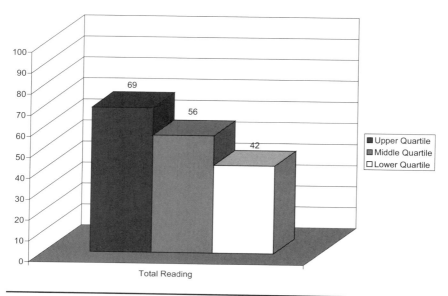

Figure 3.2 Grade four: The upper, middle, and lower quartile results for the Gates-MacGinitie total reading score.

55.48. However, utilizing the same t-test, it was discovered that one teacher's classroom scores were significantly lower than the rest, with a mean of 42.23.

Figure 3.3 compares the third-grade quartile results for the fall, winter, and spring administration of the reading fluency probes for the entire group.

The median and quartile scores for all groups had increased and the standard deviation had decreased slightly. There were no outliers in this group, and a student's t-test for each pair of the group's means demonstrated statistical significance at the .05 level between the means of the fall and winter results and the winter and spring results. Further, only one teacher in the third-grade group did not demonstrate a significant difference between the individual classroom means.

Figure 3.4 compares the fourth-grade quartile results for the fall, winter, and spring administration of the reading fluency probes for the entire group. Again the means increased, and the standard deviation decreased slightly. There was a significant difference between the means for the total group, and all teachers except one demonstrated a statistical significance between the two means in their individual classrooms.

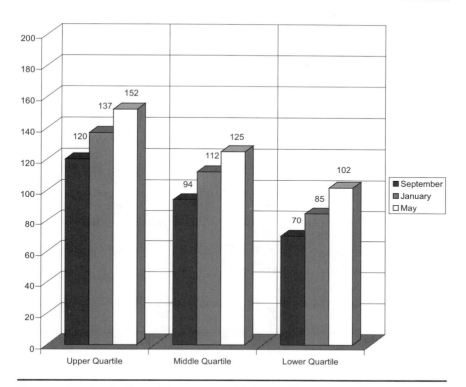

Figure 3.3   Grade three: The upper, middle, and lower quartile results from the reading fluency probes administered in September, January, and May of 2000–01.

However, in this group there were outliers, with one of the outliers being at the lower end of the scale. The number identified this student and data was given to the teacher, who used them to attempt to get special help for this child.

The individual classroom data also demonstrated that six out of the nine classroom teachers involved made continuous improvement with an increase in the mean scores and a decrease in the standard deviation.

Shinn found that fluency rates are very sensitive to changes in instruction. This is a good barometer for answering the question, "Is my instructional practice making a difference?" The other indicators utilized are not as sensitive to immediate classroom environmental changes, but they, too, must be studied to determine progress and needs.

For example, aside from looking at statistical significance between the means, how are the students in the various quartiles faring from the

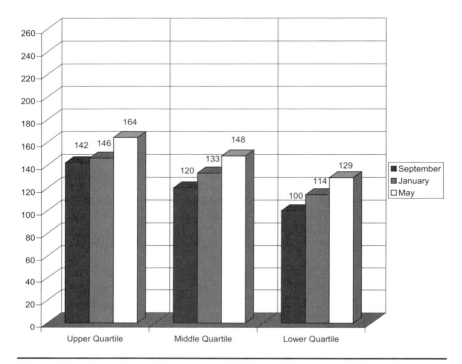

Figure 3.4   Grade four: The upper, middle, and lower quartile results for the reading fluency probes administered in September, January, and May of 2000–01.

beginning to the end of the year? The STAR reading test did not show the same significance between the means that the reading fluency probes had demonstrated for the various quartiles. Therefore, to segment the data further, the students at both grade levels who were in the upper, middle, and lower quartiles in the fall of 2000 were identified and then studied to determine their rate of growth in terms of the mean NCE scores from the fall of 2000 to the spring of 2001.

Figure 3.5 compares the improvement results for the third-grade STAR reading test administered in the fall and spring of 2000–01, and Figure 3.6 compares the same for the fourth-grade students. The federal government has identified an increase or decrease of five NCE scores as being either significant growth or significant loss.

These graphs demonstrated that for the group as a whole, especially in grade three, there was an opportunity for improvement in meeting the needs of the students who begin each year in the upper quartile. While the growth in the middle quartile was not as significant in third grade as

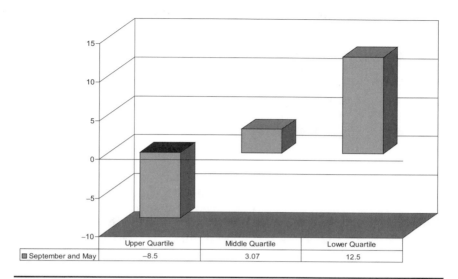

	Upper Quartile	Middle Quartile	Lower Quartile
▣ September and May	−8.5	3.07	12.5

Figure 3.5   Grade three: The mean improvement in NCE scores on the STAR reading test from September 2000–May 2001.

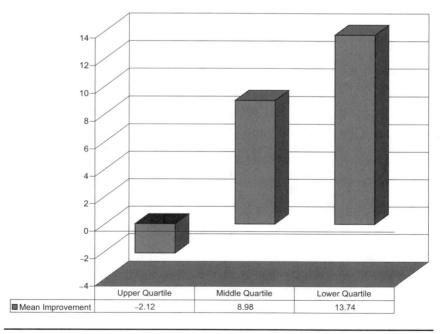

	Upper Quartile	Middle Quartile	Lower Quartile
▣ Mean Improvement	−2.12	8.98	13.74

Figure 3.6   Grade four: The mean improvement in NCE scores on the STAR reading test from September 2000–May 2001

in fourth, both demonstrated improvement. With regard to the lower quartile, both grade levels demonstrated significant growth in these students' reading achievement on the STAR reading test.

The indicator for the accelerated reader grade equivalent score was especially important because this demonstrated student reading growth based upon the sustained reading of books. Since reading is a skill that needs to be practiced, the more books read at a child's zone of proximal development is crucial to reading improvement.

Figure 3.7 demonstrates the growth for the upper, middle, and lower quartiles for the grade equivalent scores. These need to be read in terms of years and months. For example, the upper quartile fall score is 3.2. This means third grade second month. For the upper and middle quartiles, there was a significant difference between all three means. For the lower quartile, May's results were significantly higher than November's and January's. However, there was no significant difference between November and January.

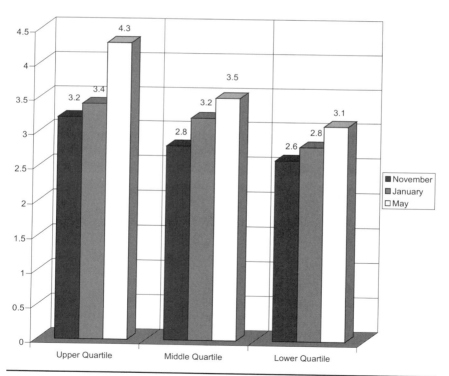

Figure 3.7   Grade three: The upper, middle, and lower quartile results for the accelerated reader grade equivalent scores.

Figure 3.8 reports the mean results in terms of months and years of growth for those students whose fall results placed them in either the upper, middle, or lower quartiles.

Figures 3.9 and 3.10 report the same results for grade four, as did Figures 3.7 and 3.8 for grade three. For grade four, the upper and middle quartiles showed significant differences in the mean between the May scores and the November and January scores. There was no significant difference between the November and January means. For the lower quartile, there were no significant differences between any of the means.

While there were significant differences in the means (with the exception of the grade four lower quartile), it was this indicator that provided the clearest opportunities for improvement in the reading instructional process. First, children of average reading ability should be expected to make nine months' growth in their grade level scores during the course of a school year. With the exception of the grade four lower quartile score, no other quartile at both grade levels demonstrated more than seven months' growth.

However, when the first reports were collected in November from the teachers who were utilizing this program, it became evident that there was already a problem. While the number of books read was not

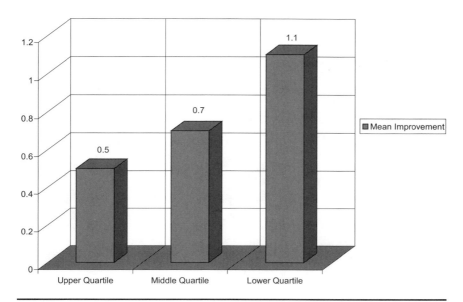

Figure 3.8   Grade three: The mean improvement for the upper, middle, and lower quartiles for the accelerated reader grade equivalent scores.

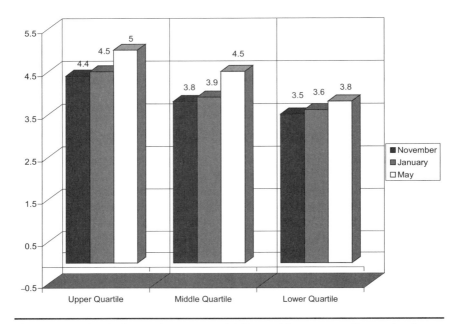

Figure 3.9 Grade four: The upper, middle, and lower quartile results for the accelerated reader grade equivalent scores.

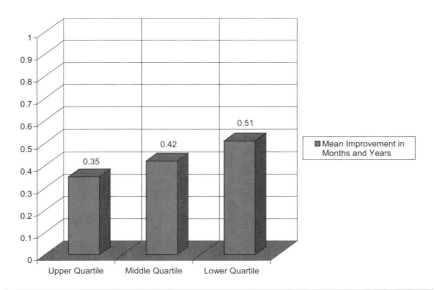

Figure 3.10 Grade four: The mean improvement for the upper, middle, and lower quartiles for the accelerated reader grade equivalent scores.

used as an indicator, the reports included this information. Many children were not reading books, because they had taken no quizzes during that time period or had taken no more than one or two quizzes. It was then discovered that only one third grade teacher had the formal accelerated reader training to implement the program.

It is the job of leadership to ensure that employees are properly trained to implement the programs they are given. In fact, Institute Training is Deming's sixth point. It was his belief that most workers were trained by other workers who themselves were not properly trained. Our hypothesis became that at the end of the year the students in the classroom of the one teacher who had received formal training would demonstrate adequate growth on the grade equivalent scores.

The hypothesis appeared to be correct, because at the end of the year this teacher's class demonstrated 1.1 years' growth. The other seven teachers' students demonstrated a range of .22 to .54 months' growth.

When the results of the grade three off-year proficiency tests and the state's grade for reading proficiency test were reported, all of the data was in place to screen statistically the indicators weighted by a passing scaled score of 217 for both groups.

Figure 3.11 indicates the grade three reading profile for success, and Figure 3.12 indicates the same for grade four. Both these profiles demonstrate the benchmarks achieved by the students who were successful on the grade three and grade four tests. Of the grade three students taking the test, 70.2 percent passed the off-year proficiency test; and 66.5 percent of the grade four students passed the State of Ohio's fourth-grade reading proficiency test. Neither group achieved the 75 percent passing rate established by the state, although some individual classrooms at both grade levels reached beyond this benchmark.

Grade Three Profile	Fall	Winter	Spring
Reading Fluency Probes	87	102	117
STAR Reading Test	51.9	56.1	56.5
Accelerated Reader Grade Equivalent Score	2.8	3.1	3.5
Gates-MacGinitie Vocabulary Subtest	49		
Gates-MacGinitie Comprehension Subtest	48		
Gates-MacGinitie Total Reading Score	49		

Figure 3.11   Grade three reading profile for success.

Grade Four Profile	Fall	Winter	Spring
Reading Fluency Probes	115	130	143
STAR Reading Test	53.9	57.8	59.9
Accelerated Reader Grade Equivalent Score	3.9	4	4.2
Gates-MacGinitie Vocabulary Subtest	51		
Gates-MacGinitie Comprehension Subtest	50		
Gates-MacGinitie Total Reading Score	51		

Figure 3.12   Grade four reading profile for success.

Designing the System: Act

The act to design the system was accomplished when the profiles were constructed. However, they still needed to be validated. Fortunately, the state changed its timeline for testing. Beginning in 2002, the Fourth Grade Guarantee would take effect, providing the state with an additional fall administration of the reading test.

This meant that the fall benchmarks could be analyzed. Since the fall accelerated reader grade equivalent scores were not available at the time results were reported, the Gates-MacGinitie indicators of vocabulary, comprehension, and total reading would be utilized as well as the results from the reading fluency probes and the STAR reading test. (See Figure 3.13.)

The fall results indicated that 53.7 percent of the students demonstrated reading proficiency on the Ohio fourth-grade Reading Proficiency Test. These test scores were then divided into two groups—students who had passed (black bars) and those who had failed (white bars)—and were compared with the five indicator test scores. Of the group (black) who had passed the Ohio test, half achieved 100 percent on the five indicator tests. Of the group (white) who failed the Ohio test, half achieved 20 percent on the five indicator tests.

The correlations between the fall scores on the Ohio fourth-grade proficiency test and the five indicators remained at 0.5 or above: Reading Fluency Probe = 0.7; Gates Vocabulary = 0.8; Gates Comprehension = 0.8; Gates Total Reading = 0.8; and the STAR reading test = 0.5.

The indicators for grade three and the remaining indicators for the winter and spring of grade four would be studied at the end of the 2002 school year.

Aside from ensuring that the benchmarks could accurately predict reading success, the profiles also had to be used by teachers. Therefore,

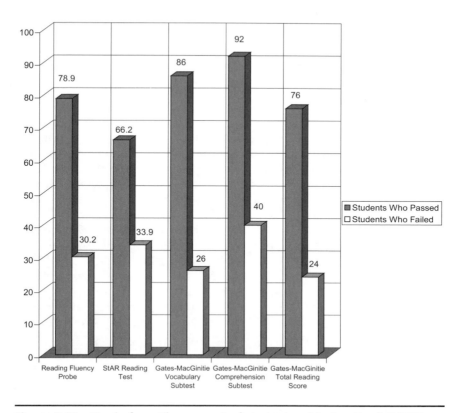

Figure 3.13 Grade four: The percent of students achieving the fall 2001 benchmarks who passed and failed the fall reading proficiency test.

as a result of what was accomplished from the grant, a Best Practice Improved Instruction Award from the Governor's Business Roundtable awarded $15,000 to continue this process. This brought the cycle back to planning. All teachers were trained in quality and the Baldrige framework. The following joint vision and mission statement was developed by the group:

Vision.

Success for all in reading

Mission Statement.

As a team of educators we will implement best practices to foster student success in reading.

The criteria for "best practices" were the following:

- Based on research
- Data driven
- Aligned to standards (district, state, national)
- Developmentally appropriate
- Learner centered

Each teacher and his/her class then developed a vision and mission statement for themselves aligned with that of the group. Their own classroom system was identified, and each teacher and his/her class developed the student's learning system, one where the students identified themselves as the workers and identified next year's teacher as an important customer.

The indicators are, of course, being administered again; teachers will now utilize the profiles to determine the needs of the group as well as individuals. During the 2001–02 school year, the knowledge gained from the profiles will be shared with parents and students who will help to develop goals for improvement.

All teachers in the group are now utilizing the accelerated reader program. However, leadership was exercised in bringing on-site formal training in this program by professional trainers based upon the grade equivalent data that were studied during the 2000–01 school year.

All teachers in the group were again given funds to spend on reading materials in the classroom, with one important difference. The mission statement aligning instruction to "best practices" must be the guiding light leading the way to the materials they purchase, as well as the analysis of their classroom data.

They will also again receive reports on the data they are collecting. However, this time there is a baseline for improvement and data comparisons can be made. Conversations at meetings now reflect the quality of instructional practices throughout the process as these teachers begin for the first time to analyze systematic, formative data.

CONCLUSION

No longer will reading improvement of students be judged by only the end-of-the-year results, which provides little more than information. With the development of the benchmarks in the reading profile for success, leaders now have the knowledge to begin making predictions. Since teachers must also become instructional leaders , they now have knowledge about the students in their rooms.

Through this information and analysis system, leaders now have objective methods to determine which teachers are in need of help. For example, the fourth-grade teacher whose Gates reading test scores were significantly lower than the rest of that group was in tears upon seeing her end-of-the-year fourth-grade proficiency test results. With only those results to study, the old conversation could have included the following:

- These reading results have to improve. Talk with teacher A whose scores were much better.
- These reading results have to improve. Find some reading staff-development opportunities to take next year and raise your scores.

This time there were data to demonstrate that this teacher's class had made remarkable improvement. The reading fluency probe results indicated that her students had made significant progress from where they had started, as did the MAZE test. Since this teacher was not then using the accelerated reader program, those results could not be utilized.

However, this teacher could only work with the class she was given; this class when compared with 150 other students had reading difficulties beyond that norm. While all teachers can benefit from professional staff development, this teacher should not just be seeking it because she is somehow deficient. In this case, the system of that school also needs to be studied to determine why those children in her class had not made sufficient progress before they entered her room. Without such an information and analysis system, this teacher's instructional expertise could be seriously misjudged, and a leader could devote time and energy in helping this one teacher when, in reality, the *system* needed to be studied.

A close look at Deming's beliefs about leadership should suggest that gaining knowledge is prerequisite. Without knowledge, leaders cannot help their people. They can only judge, and judging provides no help. Without knowledge, leaders cannot identify whether the problems their organization faces are systemic or due to individuals. Therefore, a leader cannot determine by objective methods, which employees are even in need of individual help, or whether the help that is actually required is a change in the system.

Without knowledge, leaders cannot adequately coach. Without knowledge, leaders have nothing to teach that is of any value.

One way that knowledge can be gained is through the development of in-process benchmarks in order to obtain a standard to measure the new data that is gathered in the classroom using formative indicators. In this way, leaders can begin to use data to make predictions about the future. It is with the development of an information and analysis system that instructional theories can be tested, and teachers and administrators can determine if there is quality in the process.

The administrators of today need to get themselves and their teachers out of the bunkers and establish an information and analysis system in order to search aggressively for system failure that needs to be eliminated. When they climb out, they will discover a limitless view of problem-solving opportunities.

ABOUT THE AUTHORS

Judyth Zaczkowski is in her eighteenth year as an elementary principal. She has taught graduate classes in reading for the Ohio Department of Education and Cleveland State University. She served as a senior examiner for the Ohio Award of Excellence and earned a Fellowship Award from The National Endowment for the Humanities.

Kenneth Buckley served as an elementary principal for eighteen years. In 1999, he was named a National Distinguished Principal by the National Association of Elementary School Principals. He taught graduate classes at John Carroll University and has presented papers at national and state teaching and learning conferences.

4

Student and Community Needs

Joe Thomas

INTRODUCTION

Quality management system principles govern the agreements among the people who provide goods and services to the school, the people who are employed by the school, and the people who benefit from the education provided by the school. All these people have needs the school seeks to understand, requirements that must be met, and expectations the school strives to exceed. The school focuses conservatively on the third group, which consists of students and the community (local community members, postsecondary education institutions, employers, and government agencies) as the primary customers. This chapter looks at the local community, employers, and postsecondary education as the people who need to have confidence in the school and the value of the education the school delivers. The application of quality management principles were made at Liberty Center High School and by the Penta Career Center, operating in northwest Ohio. They were selected because they are charged with assuring that graduates of the public schools have the knowledge, skill, and behavior to understand needs, meet the requirements, and exceed the expectations of society. This assurance is established and maintained by a management system that is regularly audited by an independent third party.

SETTING

The Ohio Department of Education Department of Adult Work Force Development is required to provide quality-training programs that benefit the businesses operating in the state of Ohio. To accomplish this, the Ohio Adult Workforce Development Division has developed the Ohio Adult Service Center System. Over 100 Ohio Adult Service Centers are placed strategically around the state and, of those, 20 have decided to assure their local communities and employers by registering to ISO 9001. This requires them to continue to provide programs that understand and satisfy community and employer requirements.

The high school is located in Liberty Center, OH, and the center selected for this chapter is the Penta Career Center that operates in northwest Ohio. Penta Career Center began providing consultation and training services in 1993, and works with local schools, the Ohio Adult Workforce Development Division, and the Adult Service Centers. Together they provide results of the teaching in schools of interest to the Ohio Adult Service Centers so it can supply employers with an adequately trained pool of employees. As "down-stream customers," the Ohio Adult Workforce Development organizations have a vested interest in the results of K–12 education.

This is not to suggest that local interests are the only consideration. The employers have found that to remain competitive (or just to stay in business), they need educated and trained people to produce goods and services that meet their customers' needs. To accomplish this, employers have adopted partnerships with schools to assist them in becoming more effective and as efficient as possible. In this case, the means of accomplishing this was the registration to ISO 9000. This chapter describes the registration process for the Penta Center.

THE REGISTRATION PROCESS

At first, most of the Career Centers viewed this "registration" requirement as an imposition. The initial feeling was that the customer requirements were forcing the centers to accept a thorny set of rules and regulations designed to allow absolute control of the center by the local community and employers. They accepted the conditions of ISO 9000 grudgingly at first and began to prepare for registration. In time, as they worked through the registration process, they began to accept ISO 9000 as an extremely wise decision for a way to assure the local community and employers that graduates could understand needs and meet requirements.

THE LIBERTY CENTER HIGH SCHOOL REGISTRATION

The ISO 9001 registration process was developed while working with one Ohio public school district. The registration was undertaken in order to understand how community and employer needs could be used to improve the processes of public school administration. A Penta Career Center staff member, who was trained as an ISO 9000 lead auditor, provided assistance to the district on the technical aspects of quality management principles.

Liberty Center Schools, Liberty Center, OH, began their implementation process in early 1998. At first it was ugly, because at that time ISO 9000 was not easily translated into the language used in school operations. The public schools found the language and concepts of ISO 9000 were not user-friendly and registration seemed unobtainable.

Auditors accustomed to the crisp efficiency of a well-planned manufacturing operation found the application to school operations frustrating and difficult. The school and the auditors found themselves on new ground.

Seven operational areas were found both in manufacturing a product and in providing educational service. The obstacle was to translate the requirements of each into the language of educators. The following user-friendly terms were substituted for the manufacturing and business terms:

Manufacturing and Business Terms	Public School Terms
Corporate Policy Makers	Educational Policy Makers, Boards of Education, and the School Administrators
Management	Superintendents, Principals, Directors, Program Supervisors, and Department Heads
Sales and Marketing	Development of current offerings to meet the current demands of technology and the needs of their community
Design of Product/Service (when appropriate)	Registration activities, Public Awareness Campaigns, and Course/Program Offering developments
Purchasing	Acquisition of human resources necessary to carry out the school's mission to adopt and purchase texts, materials, and equipment
Production/Service Delivery	Delivery of course content and relevant support such as support staff, course/student identification, inspection/testing, and data analysis
Shipping and Receiving	Shipping is not often found within school activities, but the receiving of purchased goods and services is

Even with this translation of terms, the initial going was slow. The only document available was the ISO 9004-2 Guideline for Service Providers. This was better than nothing, but the guidelines did not speak to the public school needs. The ISO 9004-2 guideline was also vague as to the operational aspects of the implementation process. At some period during the development of the Liberty Center implementation process, the ANSI/ASQC Z1.11 guideline for educational organizations was introduced. This provided some additional insight into the process, but again ANSI/ASQC Z1.11 did not address all of our issues. With the assistance of the president of a local registrar that provided its resources, the implementation process for the Liberty Center Quality Management System moved forward. Although the registrar provided valuable interpretations, the auditor was very careful to maintain an independent (arms length) status to avoid any appearance of a conflict of interest. Ultimately, Liberty Center High School was successful in the implementation of a quality management system based on the requirements of ISO 9002-1994. In April of 1999, Liberty Center Schools undertook and successfully completed a third-party registration audit. The registration audit identified a number of nonconformances including several document and data control issues. A few well-constructed corrective/preventive actions attained ISO 9002-1994 registration status and put the Liberty Center School's program in a competitive position with other world-class public schools. The current status is reflected in the following interview.

INTERVIEW WITH LIBERTY CENTER SCHOOLS
FEBRUARY 20, 2002

The Liberty Center ISO program is unfolding pretty much the way our consultant described it. Our first year was devoted primarily to just getting our ISO program launched. As a matter fact, the first three or four meetings were devoted entirely to just understanding the ISO language as it related to the educational service provider.

We are about halfway through our second year and we are devoting much of the time to establishing that our policies and procedures (which already have been determined to conform to ISO 9000 through the registration process) are followed. The data gathered to date (through our internal audit process) have provided administrative review of accurate data which has lead to some significant changes. The changes are primarily in the support areas of maintenance, transportation, and food service. The ISO process has allowed us to try to support activities in these areas. We have gone from a hand-to-mouth repair process to a defined preventive maintenance program. *The urgent repair situations are now covered under a standardized procedure and are now conducted with a lot more control. Operating under these conditions allows us to budget funds accurately to cover these activities.*

Our attention now is focusing on the educational process. The early returns are encouraging. We have discovered some gaps in the educational process and now have a planned method to close them.

It is anticipated that during our third year of operating a quality management system, the data provided to the administrative personnel will be such that valid determinations of change can be made and such changes will provide for successful conclusions. The need for change can now be identified and passed up through the administrative chain so that planned activities can be identified and conducted to effect these changes. This process is the result of our quality planning of procedures.

Another ISO myth that has been put to rest as a result of operating this program is that personnel, both certified and support, do not need to be thoroughly educated in the ISO process. Through our third-party surveillance audit process we are able to conclude that our processes now conform to ISO 9000, and that our staff need only know the policies and procedures that relate to them.

Another benefit of this process is that we are now able to detect trends and act on them a lot earlier and with better results than if we allowed them to run their course and had to react to them as a result of some urgent situation that would inevitably arise.

We are now engaging in preparing an application for the Baldrige award. The fact that we were registered to ISO 9000 undoubtedly was a factor when the grant for these activities was given to us.

The greatest benefit that we have identified is that throughout the entire system we have a plan to evaluate the effectiveness of activities conducted, and we have a structured means to effect changes that greatly enhance our ability to bring them to successful conclusion.

One of our greatest fears was that (and any other educational provider, for that matter) a third party would look over our operation and make judgments about how good or bad we are. Nothing could be farther from the truth. We have found that our registrar actually provides us with a service that helps us accomplish our mission. The school's objectives are achieved through mutually supportive activities. Auditors do not come in to conduct finger-pointing exercises. The fact is that these folks provide us with information that leads to opportunities for the continuous improvement of our service. Our relationship with all parties (our registrar, consultants, and staff) are viewed as professional partnerships—partnerships that work.

GETTING STARTED AT THE PENTA CENTER

The process began in 1995 with an executive briefing on ISO 9000 given to a gathering of educators and businessmen during a conference on workforce development. The following text summarized the approach: "There is a training component linked to the ISO and QS-9000 requirements that requires the ISO/QS-9000 registrant to deliver and/or receive training programs that are compatible with their own quality management systems. Such training programs are also required to be effective in their execution. Educational providers in the United States had better begin preparing to address this need." To remain competitive, manufacturers in the United States will begin to require that their suppliers (including educational providers) adopt the ISO/QS-9000 standard just as their customers require that they be certified. This training component will apply to their U.S. suppliers.

The American workforce is aging and educators really have not done much to train replacement workers to compete in a world-class environment. The European Union consumer is now asking the U.S. supplier, "How do I know that in 10 or 20 years, you will still be able to manufacture this product for me"? Tech-prep, school-to-work, and the other training programs beginning to emerge in Ohio and in the United States are going to be embraced and supported by the U.S. industrialists. Business and industry in the United States, as it always has in the past, will continue to contribute to and support education. In the future, however, there will be an even closer business/industry relationship. However, those businessmen and industrialists will start to ask, "How do we know that the providers of educational services in the USA can provide us with the world-class workforce necessary for our survival?"

IDENTIFYING THE CUSTOMERS

The job of a Diversified Industrial Training Coordinator, when working with an Ohio Career Center Adult and Continuing Education Division, is to solicit business and industry for their input on programs outside of the normal course offerings of public schools and to develop customized training programs to serve that need. One such need was to begin a program to assist business and industry with ISO 9000 implementation. After researching the requirements of ISO 9000 and taking the appropriate training programs, a consultative service was established to assist with the implementation of quality management systems that conform to the International Standard ISO 9000 published in April of 1994. During one such consultative session on vendor approval, a client asked when public schools would be registering to ISO 9000. The reply was that the subject was never really addressed. "Why not?" asked the client. There was no answer.

Four years later one Ohio public high school said it was willing to accept the challenge.

THE REGISTRATION PROCESS

After successfully registering Liberty Center Schools, the Ohio Department of Education considered registering 20 Ohio Adult Service Centers. The experience with Liberty Center identified difficulties and the need for a different approach if the registration of 20 centers was to become a reality. A partnership was formed with one of the 20 career centers.

A meaningful translation of ISO 9000 language into common terms in education continued to be a problem for the Centers' employees. A member of the U.S. delegation to ISO specializing in quality management system terminology was consulted and provided valuable assistance by translating ISO 9000 into language and concepts that were readily understood by public school employees. He spoke at various seminars and provided the group with insights into the revised ANSI/ASQC Z1.11 and ISO 9001-2000 requirements. He convinced the centers to adopt the ISO 9001-2000 standard in lieu of the 1994 version, because the ISO 9001-2000 release translated more readily into the language of public schools. By the time the Ohio Adult Service Centers were prepared to register, ISO 9001-2000 was the standard to which they registered. Implementation was supported by a series of seminars conducted over two years.

STAGES OF IMPLEMENTATION

The following is an outline of the implementation process.

Executive Briefing

The executive briefing was conducted to get top management to "buy into" the ISO program. Generally speaking, top management requires an overview of ISO 9000 that is then followed by a request to consider ISO registration. Executives attending this briefing are given an overview of what the ISO registration implementation entails and what to expect in terms of cost, both human resource and financial. ISO 9000 is reviewed on a point-by-point basis and top management determines if the process is right for them.

School administrators are also briefed so that they gain an understanding of the requirements of a quality management system based on the requirements of ANSI/ASQC Z1.11 and ISO 9001-2000 and can identify key personnel to initiate the quality management system implementation program. It is often useful to provide schools with information, timely advice, and tools to provide other educators with insight into the registration process. One such tool is the *Self Assessment for Educators.* One section is reproduced here to illustrate the tool. Other tools of this kind are also available. (See Chapter 8.)

Introduce the Standard

Key school personnel must understand what ISO 9001-2000 requires and why the requirements are in place. Using the table of contents from the quality manual, the requirements of ISO 9000 are presented, including procedures, work instructions, and records required for completing the implementation program. This exercise can generate a great deal of moaning and groaning on the part of the participants, as the process seems monumental at this point. During the training activities, myths and misconceptions regarding the requirements are removed. The reason for each of the requirements is explained in terms that are understandable to educators. The training program focuses on the reality that the ISO process and implementation of a quality management system is simply a foundation to assure that specified conditions and requirements are met. Once this is understood, the difference between the ISO requirements and current school practices is analyzed using a comprehensive "Gap Analysis."

Complete a "Gap Analysis"

Using the key administrators, a comprehensive analysis is completed to identify what steps need to be taken to align the current administration practices with the ISO 9000 requirements, based on the maturity of the existing quality management system. More mature systems have fewer gaps to fill. For this activity, a document and data control log is useful. The key administrators, who have by now developed into the implementation team, identify what documents are currently in place and what documents need to be created. When they have identified the documentation haves and have nots, the implementation team generates a comprehensive report of the analysis and presents it to the appropriate administrators, along with a time line for completion for their approval.

Document the Quality Management System

After approval of the program and time line from the administrative group, the team begins to align their applicable current documentation to conform to the requirements of ISO 9001-2000. This activity is almost always the least timely of all documentation efforts as most schools and businesses (and industries, for that matter) have very little documentation in place that readily aligns to the requirements of ISO 9001-2000.

When the alignment of in-place documentation is complete, the next step is the creation of new documents to conform to the requirements of ISO 9001-2000, as follows.

Develop and Issue a Quality (Policy) Manual

The development begins with a quality manual containing a policy for quality and an organizational chart. A quality (or policy) manual states that you shall conform to a requirement as mandated by ISO 9001-2000. The entire text of Section 4 Quality System Requirements is included here, showing conformity to section 4's requirements and identifying any procedures required.

It is important to note that most mission statements, while a necessary part of the quality manual, are at first attempt generally fluffy paragraphs that are vague and provide no means of verification of measurable objectives. If, after some time and reasonable effort, mission statements, objectives, and measures remain confused, abandonment of the quality project is tenable.

Progress toward registration is more likely when a very simple quality policy statement is drafted to outline the scope of the school registration to the requirements of ISO 9001-2000. For example:

> Quality Policy—All students will meet educational requirements that include community values and needs as a part of a registered quality system.

As you can see, the policy outlines three distinct objectives:

1st Objective: To establish and maintain a Quality Management System based on the requirements of ISO 9001-2000

2nd Objective: To assure a program of customer satisfaction

3rd Objective: To provide a means for continual improvement

These objectives are auditable and measurable. The first objective is accomplished when the department achieves registration. The second objective is verified by customer satisfaction surveys, repeat business, and recommendations of services to others. The third objective can be measured from the data generated by department meeting minutes, management reviews, and internal audits.

Create and Implement Documented Procedures

The creation of procedures is the most critical activity of all implementation events. Some attempts at this create an overabundance of paperwork. The initiated tend to write procedures that specify how the work should be done and not the way the work is done. This requires writing and rewriting and puts more writing effort into the task than is necessary. Some have tried buying a "canned" set of templates and tried to fit these to the way they do the work. This approach is almost always disastrous. While templates can be very good guides and resource material for the implementation effort, they must not be used verbatim. The guiding principle of ISO 9000 is, "Say what you do and do what you say." It is not wise to inject requirements into your quality management system that are intended to impress an auditor. This practice can in fact jeopardize your registration program. ISO does not expect procedures on how to teach how to do the work. Educators have spent a lot of time learning how to do what they do and this is verified by a certification or licensing process. Procedures should be developed to address the requirements of the standard and not go beyond that. The process is difficult enough without trying to add things or to put into place processes that are not required.

One of the more interesting procedures that educators are faced with developing is the purchasing process. In most instances the products are requested through a requisition process, passed on to administrators for approval, ordered through a purchase order program, received into a shipping/receiving department, and disseminated without incoming inspection, delivery time, or other requirements of an effective quality management system. All too often, schools order materials from whatever is available and receive it without evaluating and recording such variables as selection and approval, acceptable product, delivery time, and costs. This fairly cavalier attitude impacts the effectiveness of our whole quality management system. It is important to simplify the process for purchasing, identify checkpoints, control purchasing documents, and record the use of procedure. All persons associated with the purchasing process may need to be trained to carry out the process and to verify these activities by keeping the required records. Operating under these conditions can simplify life considerably and assure continued ability to deliver instruction as required.

Prepare Work Instructions

Work Instructions are nothing more than graphic illustrations of procedures. Work instructions are often created using the flowchart process, which is sometimes called activity process mapping. Flowcharts illustrate activities by using three or four standardized symbols that are connected with lines ending with arrowheads to show the direction of the process flow. They are simple to create and even simpler to use. Flowcharts clarify procedure requirements and are an excellent "quick" guide to the procedural process. When to do this is a matter of personal preference. Some people like to prepare the work instruction and then write a procedural narrative. Others will write the procedure and then graphically illustrate the procedure. Still others prefer to create procedures and work instructions simultaneously.

Generate Forms and Create Records

The object of the entire documentation process is to provide objective evidence to verify the effectiveness of a quality management system. This is efficiently accomplished using forms and records. The essential difference is that a record is a form that is completely filled out, signed, and dated. The signature and date become testimony that the activity has been carried out as required by stated processes and procedures. The records become objective evidence that your quality management system has been carried out and are auditable under the internal or registration audit process. Most operations have a number of forms in use and need only to create those that specifically relate to new processes initiated by the quality management system implementation program. Simply identifying these forms and records as verifications in a procedure can greatly simplify the audit process.

Initiate an Aggressive Internal Audit Program

The next step in the quality management system implementation program is to train key personnel to conduct aggressive internal audits, schedule and conduct the required internal audits, accurately summarize the audit findings, and present the summary report to the management representative. If creating procedures is the most critical part of the quality management system implementation program, internal audits are the heart and soul of the program. Aggressively conducting internal audits develops objective and reliable data with which the administrators can make accurate determinations of their processes' effectiveness and develop changes that positively impact their service delivery.

Initially, internal or registration audits are viewed by the audited as stressful events—intrusions or interferences with their respective operations. The stigma of audits is that they are faultfinding, finger-pointing, shame-on-you exercises. Most of us who have undergone audits in the past would testify to the truth in this observation. Internal audits, on the other hand, are conducted with the idea that you are doing every thing that you say you are doing. In the event that a nonconformance is identified, it should be elevated to the position of opportunity for improvement (a good thing) of the quality management system and not necessarily a finding of fault.

A good guide to the internal audit process is ANSI/ISO/ASQC Q10011, Guidelines for Quality Systems Audits, and is available through ASQ at qualitypress.asq.org. Internal audits are required by ISO 9001:2000 to be scheduled events, planned and carried out according to specified arrangements. For an example of an internal audit flowchart, see Figure 4.1.

Conduct Management Review

Utilizing the information gleaned from the internal audit, the management representatives, together with responsible administrators, review the operational aspects of the quality management system, determine the effectiveness of the quality management system activities, and make adjustments to operational procedures as necessary.

Management review is a requirement of ISO 9001-2000. Objective evidence that a management review has been conducted is required. This activity is a must before a registrar will consider a registration audit. The simplest way to accomplish this is to create a management review agenda, conduct the review, and keep minutes of the review. The minutes should reflect those activities reviewed and any conclusions or decisions made during the review. Remember, an important part of management review is a review of the quality management system. A review of the internal audit summary is an excellent way to accomplish this.

After the management review is concluded, follow-up activities must be conducted and records of the results of such follow-up activities must be maintained. The registration auditor will use these records to verify conformance and quality management system effectiveness.

Engage a Registrar

Selecting a registrar is as important an activity as creating and implementing the quality management system. It is prudent to interview several registrars to determine the fit of the registrar with the school. An

PENTA CAREER CENTER
ADULT & CONTINUING EDUCATION DIVISION
CORPORATE SERVICES GROUP _____

WORK INSTRUCTION FOR INTERNAL AUDIT	
FOR USE WITH Q.A.P.: 8.2.2	Page 1 of 1

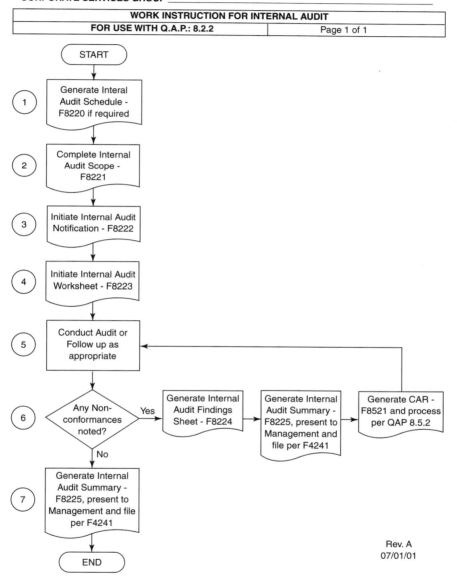

Figure 4.1 Work instruction for internal audit.

important question to ask is if the registrar has registered any educational providers. Some who have not could use your audit as a "witness" audit to add educational service providers in their scope. As more educational service providers become registered, guidelines will be developed. At this time, several registrars have been through the process, including AOQC Moody International and CRS Registrars.

LESSONS LEARNED

The major lesson learned during this process was that the application of the ISO philosophy relates to operations across a wide spectrum of activities. The authors of the ISO 9000-2000 series have taken great effort to remove any singleness of purpose from its requirements. Many organizations register to ISO 9000 as the result of a customer requirement. The companies look upon the process as a requirement, an imposition of laws and restrictions imposed by a customer wishing to obtain control over them. Others register because top management sees the process as a wise management decision. Liberty Center saw the process as an opportunity to improve their school system continuously.

Liberty Center Schools now enjoy the same benefits as business and industry with realization of increased efficiency and profitability. Educators in particular will appreciate the fact that when you look at the requirements of ISO 9001-2000 analytically, you will find a lesson plan for a course in the application of business principles. One would have a problem with an operational requirement that requires a critical look at accepting a contract to determine if you have that capacity to complete the requirements of the contract. Under the heading of what "I would do now that I didn't do then" is the creation of a model of the program before attempting to introduce the concept. This, of course, is hindsight. At the start of this program there was an idea of where to go, a standard that was primarily directed at the manufacturing industry, and a period of transition from the ISO 9000-1994 release date to the ISO 9000-2000. There is now a model developed to prepare educational providers for the registration process. Other schools developed the model over a two year period of trial and error. Penta Career Center and at least two other Ohio Adult Service Centers have successfully used this model to register their respective institutions to ISO 9001-2000.

WHERE DO WE GO FROM HERE?

A narrative of the vision for a national ANSI/ASQC Z1.11 program and how the data produced from operating a service organization quality management system will aid in the future decision-making process of educational providers. I am currently working on a program to introduce this concept on a national basis and has created a model quality management system for educational providers. It seemed to work well when the Penta Career Center used it and was registered without a nonconformance identified during the registration audit. Two other Ohio Adult Service Centers used it and went to registration. There are at least a dozen more Ohio Adult Service Centers using this model to prepare for registration by the end of the 2001–02 school year. I have had inquiries about the program from other states. Their interest is to use it to assist them with implementing an excellence (Baldrige) model to demonstrate their respective continual improvement activities. ISO registration is an excellent first step in this direction, as the data produced take their statements from the anecdotal class to the status of verifiable objective evidence, and can be used as justification information when writing their applications.

A beneficial byproduct of the quality management system is the objective data collected. Such data, when analyzed and reviewed, can provide the basis for change that is relevant and useful. The determinations made from such objective evidence will be made on fact and not surmise. This will put an end to wheel-spinning and trial-and-error approaches that plague some very good educational programs.

Another program is the Educational Program Quality Planning (EPQP). EPQP will be used to teach educators how to analyze their data accurately. Nothing will kill a project faster than drawing the wrong or inaccurate conclusions from the data collected. There are some very good tools used by the manufacturing industries to identify root causes, provide accurate solutions, and measure process (program) capability. Failure Mode and Effects Analysis (FMEA) is an excellent method to debug or to prevent bugs from entering a program. This process creates methods to identify problems long before they occur and to put preventive measures into the program that ensures a high rate of success.

ABOUT THE AUTHOR

Joe Thomas is a State of Ohio Department of Education certified consultant and trainer. He is currently employed by Penta Career Center as the Diversified Industrial Training Coordinator and Team Leader, Corporate Services Group. He served as ISO 9000 technical advisor to the Liberty Center School System, Liberty Center, Ohio.

5

Empowering the People

William N. Kiefer

INTRODUCTION

K–12 schools that are registered to the international quality management standard ISO 9001:2000 have been audited by an independent registrar who verifies that the schools meet all (over 100) requirements of the standard. These schools are subject to additional surveillance audits at least annually. If at any time a K–12 school does not meet one of the requirements, the registration is withdrawn. The community is thus assured that the results claimed are properly recorded as part of the school's quality management system.

The people are empowered in a school registered to ISO 9001 in the following ways.

Curriculum coordinators work with teachers to specify the measurable objectives in the instructional program and the metrics used to provide evidence that the objectives are being met. A formalized corrective action process is initiated by the teacher when program changes are needed. This allows teachers to use their professional knowledge and skills to design and change the learning standards for the school.

All school employees must know the quality policy and be able to relate it to their own responsibilities. This provides all employees with a central purpose and direction. School staff members receive explicit direction to ensure thorough understanding of work tasks. This reduces wasted time for teachers and staff and avoids spending energy trying to understand work requirements.

All school employees are expected to participate in internal quality audits of school and department processes. Many employees are themselves trained auditors who conduct audits. This gives employees a broader look at school and department activities and their relation to the work of others.

School employees operate the corrective and preventive action system. Corrective actions address system opportunities for improvement and preventive actions analyze trends against target objectives so changes can be planned to meet objective timelines. Experience in problem identification and analysis of causes empowers employees to seek solutions to their own problems and to improve their processes. System improvement works best in a bottom-up environment where school employees are encouraged to challenge the way things are done.

All employees must be qualified to meet their responsibilities. The school must provide objective evidence that the employees are able to meet the requirements of the tasks assigned to them. This enables employees to do their job more effectively and builds trust and confidence for the system.

Data and information are shared among employees. This provides a more substantial basis for understanding each individual's responsibility and develops ownership for the quality system.

Real quality goes beyond the ISO standard and becomes part of the school and district culture. It means that everyone takes the time to dialogue about the things that matter. The planning and implementation of quality is intended to be helpful, self-explanatory, consistent, honest, and meaningful for every employee. There are many other ways people were empowered in the following example of the 18 schools in Lancaster.

THE LANCASTER, PENNSYLVANIA SCHOOL DISTRICT

The Lancaster, Pennsylvania School District (hereafter "District") was established in 1836 and is currently overseen by a nine-member board of school directors. The boundaries of the District include Lancaster City and Lancaster Township. The blending of these two municipalities provides the District with 13.2 square miles of urban-suburban homes for nearly 69,000 people. The District schools educate over 11,000 students in 13 elementary schools, 4 middle schools, an alternative school for grades 6-12, and a high school campus with one building for grades 9-10 and one building for grades 11-12. The average age of all school buildings is 66 years. The ethnic makeup of the student population is 47.5 percent Hispanic, 26.9 percent Caucasian, 22.9 percent African-American, 2.5 percent Asian and .2 percent Native American. Twenty-two percent of the students receive special education services. Sixty-four percent of the student population qualify for free or reduced *lunch. The food service operation serves over 9000 meals per school day. The district operates with a payroll of 78 administrators, 845 professionals, and 405 service staff. Two unions represent the service staff and professional staff. The District is the eighth largest employer in Lancaster County and operated with a 2001–02 school year budget of $99.4 million. The per pupil expenditure for the 2001–02 school year was $9,100. Socio-economic challenges facing the Lancaster community include declining resources, changing demographics, increasing poverty, and increasing special education needs.*

Quality in the District

The District was the first school district in the nation to register all of its schools to the rigorous quality management standard ISO 9001:2000 (hereafter, ISO). The District focused on customer satisfaction, continuous improvement, data-driven decision making, and performance accountability. The District empowered people by improved teacher effectiveness, increased student learning, and improved employee performance. The ISO quality management system was successfully applied and the schools' performance measurably improved according to objective evidence audited by the registrar.

The goal in implementing ISO was to ensure reliable performance at each and every step of the education delivery process. The ISO management system did not dictate how the educational process should be delivered. Rather, it provided the framework to control processes, document procedures, and empower staff to satisfy requirements of customers (parents and students). The independent third-party registrar who verified that the school complied with the requirements of the standard was not concerned that each school had the "right" goals, processes, procedures, measurements, and so on, but rather how consistently and uniformly the people had implemented them across the District.

The ISO requirements are applied to and compared with actual practices a school employs to achieve its stated goals, continual improvement, and customer satisfaction. Internal audits, corrective action, and preventive action sustain the alignment of school goals and practices as situations and the environment change.

One of the most difficult things for schools is translating ISO language into concepts the people understand for all school processes. At the outset, the ISO language made quality planning difficult, because many concepts used in the standard are expressed in terms commonly used in business and industry. These same concepts needed to be expressed in terms familiar to people in K–12 schools without violating the intent of the ISO requirements. Consultants were used extensively to validate the appropriate interpretation of the ISO requirements. For example, the ISO term "product identification and traceability" was replaced with the term "control of student permanent records." The focus was on the student's (customer's) learning progress traced from kindergarten to high school graduation.

When ISO issued the 2000 version of ISO 9001, the District used this opportunity to improve its quality system to meet these new customer satisfaction requirements by taking more time to orient people to quality system concepts and to the philosophy of quality. For example, quality was defined as the ability to satisfy customers, and system was defined as the interactions among people to improve customer satisfaction. Thus, the degree of quality in the system was dependent on how well people communicated with each other in understanding the needs of students and how effectively we met the learning requirements of the students.

Significant Milestones

Implementing the ISO quality system included the following milestones:

Baseline Audit—May 9–13, 1994

Registration Audit—February 1–5, 1999

Surveillance Audit—January 31 to February 4, 2000

Surveillance Audit—February 5–9, 2001

Registration Renewal Audit—February 4–7, 2002

Registration Audit to the 2000 Standard—February 10–13, 2003

A four-year planning period before the registration audit was characterized by false starts and an insufficient appreciation of the effort required for ISO registration.

The Quality System

The original support for introducing ISO into the District was provided by Mr. Arthur K. Mann, Sr., President of the Lancaster Board of Education in 1994. Mr. Mann knew the benefits of clear expectations, customer focus, measurement of key processes, and accountability, because he had implemented ISO in his business. After receiving the support of the District's top management, a baseline study was conducted to ensure that the ISO quality system, originally designed for business, could be effectively used in K–12 schools. The baseline report was clear about the value ISO could bring to K–12 schools. Moreover, the report identified several important areas where efficiency and effectiveness of people and processes could be improved.

The Motivation

The District was determined to stop the downward spiral of student achievement and confidence in public education. It needed a structured management system to:

- Implement the strategic plan
- Implement the standards based curriculum
- Focus resources on the core business of teaching and learning
- Initiate the need for data-driven decision making
- Improve revenue through grants and taxpayer confidence
- Empower people to facilitate school-based decision making
- Improve processes through people working as teams

The Decision

The district decided that a system able to continuously improve quality throughout all schools and departments would meet the following objectives:

- Empower people to improve their processes
- Improve the quality of instruction and the quality of student work
- Improve accountability to students, parents, staff, employers, and the community
- Assure the public that the District effectively managed taxpayer money
- Provide a common plan for data management and the reporting of results

The Quality Policy

The quality policy states, "The District will continually improve teaching and learning as evidenced by high student achievement." It is understood by all district staff that this policy provides them with guidance for developing practical procedures and measures to link the District together in one system. The following system documents detail the many connections among the quality policy statement and implementation guidelines for the people in the school:

- Policy (school board guidance)
- Strategic plan (comprehensive measurable goals and objectives)

- Standard operating procedures (what needs to be done)
- Work instructions and department manuals (how people accomplish specific tasks)
- Forms, documents, and records (how people control documents and data)

The quality policy became the strategic planning guide for people to develop their procedures and practices. It became the foundation for the development of the standard operating procedures that explain "what" people do, the work instructions that explain "how" it is done, and internal audits that check to see if, in fact, what is done is consistent with the documentation. Essentially this followed Shewhart's Plan-Do-Check-Act Cycle. The people serving as teams planned what needed to be accomplished, how it needed to be accomplished, checked if it was accomplished, and acted to make appropriate changes as necessary.

The Documentation System

The District's quality manual describes how the management system works overall. Each school and department developed quality manual statements to comply with the requirements of the standard. These statements became the foundation for the standard operating procedures (SOPs) that described the work people needed to accomplish to meet the requirements of the statements in the quality manual. Work instructions and department manuals were developed to describe how people got the work done. During this process the focus was on the core business of teaching and learning, effective school planning, empowering people, measurement, and accountability. The principles for school quality included:

- Leaving no child behind
- Rigorous academic work
- High expectations and support
- Progress in teaching and learning results
- Teamwork at the school and district level
- Partnerships with businesses and the community
- Accountability for results

The capacity of the system grew as people thoughtfully assessed their needs and planned the necessary improvements to their processes. The corrective action process encouraged people to identify and report opportunities for improvements in the system. By enhancing each individual's involvement, continuous process improvement grew and people became empowered to make changes. Staff thought critically about their practices and sought improvements in the efficiency and effectiveness of their work. Effective processes were retained; processes needing improvement were strengthened; ineffective processes were discarded. People began to realize that the quality system was not another task, it was simply adding value to the work they were already doing. The quality system belonged to the people doing the work of the District.

System Integration

The innovative practices were easily integrated into the quality system. The ISO framework provided the structure to connect the reform initiatives to the system. Taken together, the reforms and the quality system set up a method to innovate and design metrics to evaluate the value of new practices. Data and objective evidence were produced to meet the requirements of the quality system and help build a data-driven process and reporting structure. The quality policy and supporting documents developed employee understanding for the changes and linked employee and management accountability. Ultimately, the line of accountability was clearly identified. This clarity demanded the following:

- Objectivity and a culture of honesty
- Critical feedback and support
- A consistent purpose that the entire staff struggled daily to maintain

The clarity provided a working environment in which each staff member understood that systemic change was a significant part of the quality initiative.

Linking Process Improvement and Documentation

The implementation process began with a comprehensive project plan designed to anticipate every twist and turn that might be encountered as the quality journey unfolded. This was quickly discarded as unworkable by the staff and replaced with process-writing teams who connected the system requirements to the people responsible to implement the required processes. The use of cross-functional teams to describe and document procedures generated consistent best practices across the District. Process-writing teams benefited from training in understanding systems thinking and process improvement techniques. The power of the system was demonstrated by how well it was implemented by the people in the schools and departments. Implementing a new system was not as easy as it first seemed. It was challenging work to continue checking that tasks were done as planned. If they were not, either the plan or the task needed to be adjusted and checked again until it was done right. Sustaining improvements required continual coaching and mentoring to bring people along slowly when necessary or more rapidly once they had the requisite understanding. Clearly, it was equally as important to understand how to implement the system as it was to understand the system.

The role of the person who served as the quality manager was to facilitate the best thinking among the staff, not to create documents in isolation. The most effective documentation associated with the quality system came as a result of a process involving people in planning and implementation. People found that it was important to go through the process of writing their own documents to clarify their thinking and recognize opportunities for improvement. A significant upfront investment in systems thinking, processing opportunities for improvement, and problem solving produced a substantial return in time and effectiveness in the long term.

Staff teams, including people who eventually implemented the procedures, were best at writing the procedures. More detailed work instructions, department manuals, and handbooks at each school and/or department supported District procedures by explaining how processes were to be completed. Because of the unique circumstances of each school or department, actual procedures or content varied. Procedures were tailored to be explicit, helpful, and self-explanatory and were reviewed from the point of view of those required to do the work. The staff could significantly increase the effectiveness of their processes, improve relationships, and increase the level of trust among their colleagues when they had clearly written, consistently applied, and publicly shared processes. Just as important, improved processes needed to be institutionalized by documented procedures and staff training.

Customer Satisfaction

An improvement plan without customer input is a fool's mission that may never meet quality system requirements. The successful leaders accepted the view that the primary measure was of customer satisfaction. Thus the overall objective in developing improvement plans was to increase customer satisfaction. Leaders identified their specific customers, determined customer requirements, and defined how they would measure satisfaction. Each school records customer concerns and surveys its customers annually.

A districtwide customer satisfaction survey was conducted to measure community satisfaction with the strategic direction, leadership, communications, responsiveness, programs, curriculum, instruction, discipline, and utilization of facilities. The survey included a "comments section" for personal responses. The plan was to obtain baseline data relative to the public's perception of how well the District was performing. Three thousand individuals were randomly selected from the tax rolls and sent a survey during the first week of November 2000. Three hundred thirty-five completed surveys were returned and tabulated. Follow-up surveys are planned to develop trend data and identify specific areas for improvement actions.

Implementing the Quality System

The much-used quality phrase "Say what you do, do what you say, and prove it" became the "watchword" for the work of the school district, and the ISO quality standard became the framework for building a planning system of continuous improvement. As teams of administrators, teachers, and support personnel began reviewing their current practices and establishing clearly defined practices, communication between and among schools and departments improved. Implementation required the participation of all employees. School leaders found that they could not abdicate their responsibility for quality. It became clear that only when the leaders effectively executed appropriate management of the system could they realize the enthusiasm and creativity of their staff. Leaders who were successful system implementers became teachers and coaches of quality in their school or department. ISO provided the structure in which the schools and departments planned improvement efforts. Those who made decisions in a more inclusive atmosphere brought focus and purpose to their staff. Previously, the District was a system of firefighters. It was expert at putting out fires and felt pretty good about the ability to take on "three-alarm" challenges with great skill. It's hard to think about and look deeply into something when you are constantly putting out fires, yet putting out fires was exactly what the work was about: fixing things, never asking the question about improving things in the first place. The ISO element of corrective action took us to another level of thinking. The idea of corrective action was to drive the thinking deeper, to find the root causes of the fire and apply system methods to keep it from recurring.

Internal Auditing

Internal quality audits were initiated to provide continuous review of progress and compliance to the standard. Internal audit teams were trained in the requirements of the standard, corrective action processes, root cause analysis, observation techniques, interviewing techniques, confidentiality, and recording and reporting nonconformances. It became evident that both individuals being audited and those doing the auditing were learning more about quality and the system. Internal quality audits immediately began increasing employee understanding. The benefits of the internal auditing process included:

- Verifying compliance to requirements
- Identifying improvement opportunities
- Exercising the corrective action process

Additionally, best practices found at one school were duplicated by the audit team and taken back to their own school. Confidence in the system grew, and school personnel were soon expressing their ideas on the characteristics of how the quality system was applicable to their work. They viewed their system as:

- A framework that blended innovation with system standards
- A structure to improve dialogue between schools and departments
- A balance between goals and practices
- A process to measure school objectives
- A process for employee-initiated continuous improvement

Implementation Steps

Phase I (Baseline Assessment). The baseline audit was a detailed systems audit comparing the current practices of each school and department with all ISO elements. This was the first quality audit of a public school system and it determined that, indeed, the rigor of a quality standard such as ISO could be used effectively in a school district. The audit identified opportunities for process improvements and efficiencies that would realize cost savings.

Phase II (Orientation). The orientation was a half-day leadership overview workshop for board members, superintendent, senior staff, and school principals. The workshop included the basic requirements of the standard, operational requirements, system objectives, and planning steps.

Phase III (Training). Training consisted of a one-day implementation workshop to educate and train staff to understand the quality system and their role in implementing quality; a one-day documentation workshop to educate and train personnel in formatting and consistency techniques for controlling documents, records, and forms; and a one-day internal auditor workshop to develop quality system auditors knowledgeable in the preparation, execution, and reporting of internal audits.

Phase IV (Process Writing Teams). Process-writing teams were consultant-led teams that planned and deliberated over each quality manual statement and every standard operating procedure (SOP). This process helped each school and department leader better understand systems thinking and process planning. Against this backdrop of professional development, district-writing teams charted work processes, wrote documents, and made decisions for their quality system. As staff became more skilled at quality system activities, each important operational process was flowcharted or documented as standard operating procedures (SOPs). The District's top management people, including the superintendent and directorates, maintained the quality manual and standard operating procedures as follows:

Management Review—Superintendent

Quality System—Superintendent

Contract Review—Deputy Superintendent

Design Control—Director of Teaching and Learning

Design Changes—Director of Teaching and Learning

Writing a Controlled Document—Director of Planning and Quality Systems

Control of Quality System Documents—Director of Planning and Quality Systems

Control of Public Domain Documents—Director of planning and Quality Systems

Control of School/Department Documents—Director of Planning and Quality Systems

Control of School/Department Forms—Director of Planning and Quality Systems

Purchasing—Director of Finance and Administration

Preferred Vendors List—Director of Finance and Administration

Issuance of Purchase Orders—Director of Finance and Administration

Control of Student Materials—Deputy Superintendent

Control of Student Records—Deputy Superintendent

Process Control (teaching)—Director of Teaching and Learning

Process Control (learning)—Director of Teaching and Learning

Assessment—Director of Teaching and Learning

Materials and Services—Director of Teaching and Learning

Validity and Reliability of Assessments—Director of Teaching and Learning

Control of Measuring Devices—Director of Teaching and Learning

Recording and Reporting of Student Achievement—Director of Teaching and Learning

Control of Nonconformance—Superintendent

Corrective Action—Superintendent

Customer Complaints—Director of Human Resources

Preventive Action—Deputy Superintendent

Handling, Storage, and so on—Director of Finance and Administration

Discipline—Deputy Superintendent

Control of Records—Director of Planning and Quality Systems

Control of School/Department Records—Director of Planning and Quality Systems

Internal Audits—Director of Planning and Quality Systems

Staff Development—Director of Teaching and Learning

Transcripts—Director of Planning and Quality Systems

Statistical Techniques—Superintendent

Data Management—Superintendent

Standards in Practice—Director of Teaching and Learning

Continual Improvement—Superintendent

Improvement Plans—Superintendent

Phase V (Mentoring). Interaction and coaching between the consultant and school district people to problem solve language translation and planning issues constituted the mentoring phase. Progress was slow and arduous but momentum gained as the people's understanding increased. Periodic project audits were initiated to get a second-party look at progress, gaps in meeting system requirements, and staff training. These periodic checks were used to review and verify if processes and documents were accurate, authentic, complete, and effective. Moreover, these midpoint audits measured the District's readiness to withstand for the rigors of a third- party registration audit.

Phase VI (Readiness for the Registration Audit). Readiness was the final dress rehearsal in preparation for the registration audit. A team of qualified auditors reviewed the total system implementation to identify areas needing to be addressed prior to the third-party registration audit.

Phase VII (The 2000 Revision). The 2000 revision of the ISO standard is much more appropriate for public education. The language is clearer and diversification of the elements more closely mirrors the complexity of a social institution such as public education. New standard operating procedures (SOPs) had to be developed to address continuous improvement, customer satisfaction, and data management. Because of the learning that had taken place since the registration audit in 1999, the District took this opportunity to do a complete rewrite of the quality manual and a thorough review of all SOPs. Moreover, the SOP format was changed so everyone would know the new 2000 procedures at a glance.

The Quality System in Action

The following example describes how the quality system was used to build practical solutions to systems issues.

Pennsylvania established a standard testing assessment for each school district and publicly released the results. To meet these new requirements and improve teaching and learning, the District restructured the curriculum and designed a more robust professional development plan. The quality system process for design inputs, outputs, review, verification, validation, and changes was instituted to ensure the designs met the requirements of the quality standard. After a period of study, the redesigned curriculum was launched. Following implementation, internal audit teams interviewed teachers regarding the effectiveness of the implementation. Some teachers submitted corrective actions, and school principals reported preventive actions during mid-year reviews with the superintendent. Additionally, annual school improvement plans were updated with new processes and updated metrics. Following the use of systemic processes and explicit procedures, the new curriculum improved teacher and parent satisfaction.

Observed Benefits

A system focused on core processes

Consistency in program implementation

Available method to implement best practices

Disciplined approach to responsibility and accountability

Better understanding of status with measured results

Actions resulting from trend analysis

Data-driven decision making

Process for systematic continuous improvement

Cost savings/efficiencies

Customer service orientation

Increased staff capacity and empowerment

Cultural and attitudinal shift

Results

The ISO requirement for statistical techniques was interpreted as data management for the district's quality system. Implementing a system of data management meant that the important data elements had to be measured. It was necessary to establish a systems approach to the reporting of performance indicators that was consistent, reliable, and available in real-time for the purpose of making decisions at the District, school, and department levels. To accomplish this, the district established a standard operating procedure (SOP) for data management. More importantly, the data management indicators are repeated in the SOPs for management review, preventive action, and improvement. The system is connected and aligned across all data elements identified in the strategic plan. At this point, an annual community report was published to make the data public. Some of the report includes the following results in the area of student achievement and attendance.

Student Achievement

The student achievement in core subjects was measured using student performance in reading and mathematics on the Pennsylvania System of School Assessment (PSSA). There are four categories: top (advanced), high middle (proficient), low middle (basic) and bottom (below basic). In 1998 many of the students were not meeting basic standards. In 2001 a change in the PSSA scoring required higher scores for students to move into the advanced and proficient levels. Using 2000 criteria to better illustrate the significance of the increase in student achievement, total district scores in math and reading show 37 percent of students in the bottom quartile in 2001 compared to 43 percent in 2000, 46 percent in 1999 and 51 percent in 1998, demonstrating a 14 percentage point reduction in students scoring below basic skills.

Attendance

Attendance is also a key factor in raising student achievement. Student attendance in many of the schools has risen significantly, placing them at or above their attendance goal. Attendance in some schools, however, needed to improve. The schools have now instituted a stronger attendance and tardy policy for all students from kindergarten through high school. Backed by a new Standards of Conduct adopted by the School Board, administrators, teachers, and community partners have established the expectation that all students must be at school on time, everyday. The standards are high and the consequences tough, but to prepare students for the future schools are teaching them early the importance of responsibility and punctuality.

Other Improvements

Special Education Medicaid Revenue increased $500,000

Grants increased by $7 million annually

The cost of procurement was reduced with electronic purchasing

Parent complaints and concerns were quickly addressed

Student records transfer time was reduced

The net effect on teaching and learning in the 1997–98 school year was that 635 students did not matriculate because of their inability to demonstrate mastery of learning standards. Subsequent extended learning opportunities (summer school) were provided, and most of these children moved forward. Clear, unequivocal standards, however, are now established for student performance.

Evaluation by the Empowered People

The District successfully completed a third-party registration audit the first week of February 1999. The registration to the ISO quality standard ensures that the District:

1. Says what it does through the documentation of the policies and procedures
2. Does what is said through day-to-day work processes
3. Proves it through ongoing audits and metrics
4. Continually improves processes through employee involvement in the corrective action process

The quality system has built the professional and organizational capacity of the District. It has made the district more responsive as a system and increased operational effectiveness. ISO has proven a valuable tool to empower school staff to own their destiny through the quality system. The practical effect of the quality system is illustrated in the following remarks from the people who were empowered by the quality management system:

- "Service people are buying into the quality statement—they are part of the learning process."
- "Internal audit teams help people find out what is going on in other places."
- "The quality system builds appreciation for other job functions."
- "The quality system has come at a critical time in the school district— major restructuring, site based decision making."
- "The quality system gives us a way to track ongoing ideas."
- "The best thing the District does is audits—it gets us out there to learn other functions and spread the message to other people."
- "The quality system has awakened us to the potential we really have."
- "The quality system has proven to be the best structure to implement significant change."

Each future application will undoubtedly vary; however, the process of organizing a quality system will always help create a lasting institutional framework of cause and effect. ISO has become a useful tool for building staff capacity, responsibility, and accountability at every level of the school. It has formed a basic building block for school teamwork. It has brought together instructional and non-instructional personnel in a practical way to achieve a unified vision of quality for the children. It has helped knit together a network of student-centered supports and services."

WHAT THE NATION WANTS . . .
QUALITY SCHOOLS—NO EXCUSES!

One way businesses are staying competitive is by registering their businesses to ISO. K–12 schools must also be competitive. Public education provides the foundation to study one's culture and heritage by teaching our youth to read, compute, think critically, problem solve, and enjoy the arts. Ultimately, K–12 education provides students with the skills needed to lead successful and fulfilled lives as productive citizens.

Applying ISO to education will result in higher student achievement, improvements in teaching effectiveness, and a reduction in the cost of educating our children. Our nation wants results. Our children deserve nothing less than the best education we can deliver. No excuses!

ABOUT THE AUTHOR

William N. Kiefer, Ed.D. has been a teacher, psychologist, department head, elementary principal, secondary principal, and cabinet-level administrator. Currently, he is the Director of Planning and Quality Systems for the School District of Lancaster, Pennsylvania.

Under Dr. Kiefer's leadership, Lancaster was the first U.S. school district to be registered to the ISO 9001 quality standard.

6

Utilizing Partnerships

Robert Kattman

INTRODUCTION

In 1994 a suburban Milwaukee school district began its quality journey with a strategic plan that identified the creation of academic standards with aligned assessments as the most important goal in its quest to continually improve student learning. The district serves students in four-year-old kindergarten through grade eight. It is one of three K–8 districts that feed into a common, union high school. Because of the K–8/union high school arrangement, the district recognized early on that it would have to establish key partnerships with the other districts if its goal was to be realized. Further, because of the small size and limited staffing of each district, a partnership would also have to be developed with an agency knowledgeable in the standards movement.

Today the school district is well along the way to having a mature quality system with a standards-based educational program. The maturing of this district's quality system over seven years and the development of partnerships which enabled it to reach its goals provides an example of focused efforts utilizing a quality approach. The measured results and the lessons learned during the past seven years are presented from the superintendent's perspective.

THE CONTEXT

The district has a long history of using a continuous progress strategy for student learning based on its design of educational programs and curricula. It had a well-established reputation for academic excellence and the high school has ACT test scores that are among the highest in the state. A quality management system was introduced in 1994 to maintain this measure of academic excellence while improving the learning of each student. This is reasonable in a state with a history of strong local control that encouraged districts to design educational programs to meet community requirements and to exceed their expectations. Local control had begun to diminish in the early 1990s with the approval of legislation that controlled both the amount of revenue schools could raise and the compensation increases employees could receive. The move toward state control of schools accelerated in 1996 when the state assumed two-thirds of the statewide costs of K–12 education.

In 1996, two years after the district determined the need for standards and assessments, the legislature passed laws requiring the development of academic standards and assessments. The state's effort ran parallel to the work in the district and significantly affected its efforts. Although the concept of state standards is appropriate, the process for their development at the state level was political and fraught with problems and inconsistencies. For example, the state adopted a form of the Terra Nova, a norm-referenced test developed by CTB-McGraw Hill, to assess students in grades four, eight, and 10. Two years after the test was adopted, academic standards were developed with no attempt to align the standards to the test. The state intended to use this system to determine whether or not student in grades four and eight would be promoted to the next grade. In addition, sometime after 2004 a yet-to-be developed high school graduation exam will be used to determine whether or not a student will be awarded a high school diploma. The district's quality system needed to be robust enough to survive in this environment.

THE QUALITY SYSTEM

Working in this environment, the district adopted eight principles of quality management, based on the Baldrige core values, to guide the school's system of accountability designed to continually improve learning processes for students. The following quality management principles as discussed in chapter 1 were adopted by the district.

Customer Focus

The district schools exist to prepare students to become successful adults. Therefore, its actions must be based on a continuing understanding of what the students, their parents, and society believe is required for their success. The use of a balanced composite of performance measures provides an effective means to communicate short- and long-term priorities, to monitor performance, and to marshal support for improving results.

Leadership

Alignment of people's efforts with the district's mission, beliefs, and strategic goals is required to create a unity of purpose. Therefore, its leaders must establish direction, clear and visible values, and high expectations to guide all the decisions of the organization. They must create strategies, systems, and methods for achieving excellence, stimulating innovation, and building knowledge and capabilities through the development of the entire workforce. They must encourage participation, learning, innovation, and creativity by all employees.

Involvement of People

The school district's success depends on the knowledge, skills, creativity, and motivation of its workforce. Therefore, the district must invest in the education, training, and opportunities for continuing growth for all employees. These opportunities need to be tailored to a diverse work force and to flexible, high-performance work practices.

Process Approach

Desired results are achieved more efficiently when the interdependence of the resources and activities that influence them can be identified and managed as processes. Focusing on the development of well-designed processes that contribute directly to continuously improving student learning is essential to achieve the district's mission.

Systems Approach

The school district is a single system of interrelated processes. Understanding the relationship of any one process to the whole and that action taken in one process affects all other processes is essential to managing the system. The effectiveness and efficiency of a school district depends upon the extent to which it can identify, understand, and manage its processes as a connected system.

Continual Improvement

Achieving the highest levels of performance requires that the school district has a well-executed approach to continuous improvement. Therefore, improvement and learning must be a regular part of daily work; practiced at the individual, team, and organizational levels; used to eliminate problems at their sources; and be driven by opportunities to make both incremental and breakthrough improvement.

Factual Approach to Decision Making

Data and information are required to measure and improve a school district's performance. The measures selected should best represent the factors that lead to improved student performance, customer satisfaction, and operational and financial performance.

Mutually Beneficial Partnerships

Partnerships enhance the organization by blending the school district's core competencies with the complementary strengths of its internal and external partners. Therefore, the school district, in cooperation with its partners, must develop long-term objectives to create the basis for mutual investment that enhances overall capability and increases value for each member of the partnership.

THE MOTIVATION AND RESISTANCE

The strategic goal to develop academic standards and assessments arose from the district's desire to increase the academic results achieved by students. To accomplish such improvement, it was recognized that changes needed to be made in the areas of planning and instruction, and that quality management principles could provide the direction for these changes. The system in place included well-designed curricula, well-trained teachers, and the best available learning materials. Certainly the opportunity for students to learn existed. Results from national norm-referenced tests such as the Iowa Test of Basic Skills indicated that its students were doing very well. Administrators and curriculum personnel, however, had several nagging concerns. When different instructional strategies were used, there were no methods to determine whether the effect was positive or negative. In parent-teacher conferences, teachers and parents consistently agreed that students should take greater responsibility for their own learning, but there was little evidence that this was occurring. Parents wanted the most appropriate high school placement for their student, yet the elementary school staff could not readily explain why and how students were placed in high school.

Upon analysis it was clear that goals for student learning were not clear, that there was no way to measure what students actually knew and were able to do, and that the high school placement procedures were not linked to instruction students received in the elementary schools. To address these problems, the district realized that it needed to:

1. Define what students were expected to know and be able to do
2. Develop an assessment system that would provide data on both student achievement and instructional effect
3. Develop a process for continual improvement of all system elements

As part of its quality system effort, the district recognized that staff members were empowered toward continual improvement when they clearly understood expectations, had control of the processes for which they had responsibility, received feedback about their work, and were given the opportunity to grow professionally. The district believed that these same principles held true for students and would enable students to take greater responsibility for their own learning. They needed to have clear learning goals, specific feedback about their work, and certainly many opportunities to grow academically. This was especially true in regard to the expectations for high school entrance and placement.

Continuous improvement efforts in the district were also dependent upon reworking its approaches toward staff development. Past practices toward school improvement were characterized by fragmented, insufficient attempts to bring about change. Many of the in-service initiatives were tied to methods that were perceived as add-ons or strategies to revitalize and reform individual teacher behaviors. The missing link in the training process was a clear, coherent plan for systemic change where curriculum and instruction changes were linked to student performance. Its need for improvement transcended defining clear learning goals and developing effective data management techniques. The district needed to develop a process to increase the knowledge and skill levels of teachers to integrate assessment results into the very fabric of lesson and unit planning. Teacher and student empowerment were inextricably linked to making decisions about instruction and learning strategies based on meaningful and timely performance data.

SETTING THE STAGE

The strong commitment of the district to standards development and performance assessments was initially challenged by the enormity of the task and by the knowledge that identified problems would not be solved unless the high school and other elementary districts in the high school area were part of the process. Although the three elementary feeder districts have much in common and work cooperatively in many instances, they were also fiercely independent. As a result, each elementary district developed its own program of instruction which, while sharing many attributes, created differences among student preparation as they entered the high school. Given the identified needs and the concern of parents about high school entrance, it was not surprising that the eighth to ninth grade transition became the primary focus for discussion among the districts about standards development.

The first task was convincing the other districts to join in a partnership to address the issues. Agreeing to be part of the process was in reality a major systemic change. Each district was asked to adopt a common purpose, to focus organizational energy on the project, and to promote team learning. To be successful, the process of change had to be managed at all levels of consortium, district, and building. Because of a unique arrangement wherein the district shares its district-level administration with one of the other elementary districts, a second district was quickly brought on board and the high school was soon added as administration saw the value of the project. The final district initially became only peripherally involved and did not become a full partner until the second year of the project. The loose agreement that was initially reached for all four of the districts to become part of the project turned into a firm commitment when a federal Goals 2000 application was funded in the amount of $60,000 to support the project in its first year. The Goals 2000 grant was subsequently renewed for each of the next five years, providing between $60,000 and $80,000 per year to support the project.

As the consortium was being formed, it quickly realized that the district did not have the expertise in standards and assessments required to address the problem. Another partner was needed. The Mid-continental Regional Education Laboratory (McREL) was identified as the ideal partner. The district was already involved with McREL through the use of Dimensions of Learning. McREL also served as a national clearinghouse for information on standards, and had a team of consultants knowledgeable in the development and use of standards at the school-district level. A contract was developed with McREL to provide the following services:

1. A synthesis of national standards to serve as a knowledge base for the project
2. Design criteria for standards, benchmarks, and assessments
3. A review of consortium-adopted standards
4. Training for staff in developing standards and assessments
5. Advice to the project leaders about quality control issues
6. Training for district personnel to manage the standards and assessment-development process in the local districts

Forming a consortium and finding a credible consultant were two formidable obstacles. Another was obtaining the commitment of all consortium members to make this project a key component of their strategic plan for a minimum of five years. Project success required more than the development of standards and related assessments. It also demanded extensive staff training, time for unit planning, action research, data analysis, and product revision and refinement. Only if these requirements were met would changes become part of each district's culture of excellence.

INITIATING THE PROJECT

Change never comes easily and the process for the development of standards and assessments for the four districts proved to be no exception. Although standing committees existed in each subject area to discuss the transition process from middle school to high school, teachers and administrators alike had to begin thinking differently. The development of standards and assessments required a systems approach rather than that of an individual practitioner. It required a constructivist view of learning rather than a transmission of knowledge viewpoint.

Curricula had to be designed to reflect what students learn rather than what teachers teach. And, perhaps most importantly, it had to be driven by data indicating what students actually know and are able to do rather than by ranking and labeling students.

To plan and guide the project, a coordinating committee was formed of curriculum specialists from each district and department chairs from the high school. The coordinating committee set guidelines for, and served as a liaison with, cross-district curriculum teams to ensure grassroots involvement in the development, refinement, and implementation of a standards-based program in each district. The involvement of frontline teachers in the development of the standards and assessments was deemed essential to the process. Only by involving them in the total process would the districts create the ownership necessary to make the project a success.

The project was designed to focus school improvement through a standards-based instruction and assessment model. The first step was to establish clear expectations for student achievement. These standards and benchmarks would provide a clear and discriminating target for instructional planning. The second step was to provide valid and reliable assessment instruments to measure student progress toward reaching program standards. The assessments were the key element for the whole process, providing various stakeholders, teachers, students, parents, administrators, and interested community members with reliable and meaningful data to judge program effectiveness. The third step was to use data from the standards assessment program to determine school and district improvement goals.

The model was designed to provide two levels of data. The first level was student-centered. School structures and systems would be built to monitor individual student achievement with respect to the identified standards and benchmarks. Students, parents, and teachers would receive a diagnostic profile based on student performance. In addition to student performance, the system would provide specific criteria and exemplars for performance standards to guide student performance goal setting. The second level was school and district performance. Through norm- and criterion-referenced data, school and district diagnostic profiles would be built. These profiles would enable each district to identify relative program strengths and weaknesses, which in turn would help each district to establish data-driven school improvement initiatives directly related to student achievement.

THE FIRST YEAR

In the fall of 1996, the cross-district curriculum teams in the areas of language arts, mathematics, science, and social studies began their work. The specific goals of the project included:

- Developing local content standards and benchmarks in each curriculum area and standards for lifelong learning
- Providing resources for teachers to develop knowledge and skills relative to standards-based education and performance-based measures of assessment
- Developing school processes that implement and monitor student achievement with respect to the identified standards and benchmarks
- Providing coordination of staff development efforts in the areas of standards, assessments, the Dimensions of Learning model, and other instructional techniques
- Emphasizing thinking skills as an integral part of the standards, assessments, and instruction
- Providing program equity in and among all schools

Guided by curriculum resource personnel from each district and McREL consultants, each cross-district curriculum team struggled with the change in viewpoint as they formed into a working group. These efforts were complicated by the need to arrive at a common format for standards and benchmarks. Many sets of goals and standards published by various organizations and institutions were examined and synthesized. From these resources, specific criteria were developed to define clearly the format and level of specificity required to design the standards and benchmarks. Once the design specifications were agreed upon, each team had to learn to create learner expectations to meet these criteria. To aid this process, experts at McREL reviewed drafts of the standards and benchmarks. The process was very frustrating at first and required several drafts, but became quite rewarding as each team mastered the process and was able to celebrate initial success.

By the end of the 1996-97 school year, work was well under way. The cross-district curriculum teams had developed a common vision, struggled through the development of several drafts of standards and benchmarks, and initiated the developmental work on the assessment portion of the project. The teams in each subject area completed documents detailing eighth-grade content standards and benchmarks for their respective curriculum areas. These documents exceeded original expectations by detailing benchmarks for a grade-level span (grades 6–8) rather than a single grade level (grade eight). The documents were then processed, analyzed, and returned to the consortium by the project technical consultant (McREL). Various staff members read and assessed the proposed standards and benchmarks. This staff input was used to revise and refine every document before presenting them to each consortium school board.

During the summer of 1997, members of the cross-district curriculum teams were trained to assist other teachers in their respective districts to develop benchmarks and assessments at grades K–2, 3–5, and 9–12. The curriculum teams were also trained how to design assessments that incorporate lifelong learning standards with the content standards. Lifelong learning standards include knowledge and skills in the areas of complex thinking, information processing, communication, and collaboration.

THE SECOND YEAR

During the 1997-98 school year, consortium activities operated on two levels. New cross-district teams were created to review the completed grade 6–8 exit standards and determine connected benchmarks for grades 3–5 and grade 9. At the same time the initial cross-district curriculum teams:

1. Designed the assessment program for the 6–8 grade standards
2. Piloted performance assessments for eighth grade
3. Continued to revise and refine the grade 6–8 benchmarks and assessments

4. Developed a prototype system for scoring, recording, reporting out assessment results
5. Began to align benchmarks with other testing programs (for example, Wisconsin Department of Public Instruction and the National Assessment of Educational Progress)

McREL continued to serve as the technical advisor for both levels. McREL coached the members of the initial cross-district teams in the training of the new committees, processed and critiqued all documents, and provided assessment templates and exemplars for work at grades 3–5 and 9. McREL also oversaw the development and piloting of assessments, provided training and models for the prototype report-out system, and gave technical advice for the benchmark alignment process.

Work also began within districts to provide in-service training for teachers on a Dimensions of Learning unit planning model. The Dimensions of Learning model features a decision-making matrix that integrates complex thinking, information processing, communication, and collaboration skills into instructional planning. This type of training is necessary for teachers to recognize the connection between assessment methods and teaching strategies. Once the standards-based program is fully implemented, districts will be responsible for assessing and reporting on student progress for each agreed-upon benchmark. Teachers will serve as the chief agent for the collection of standards data. In order to do this, they will need a whole repertoire of assessment techniques to gather data and make judgments related to student performance.

In addition to Dimensions of Learning training, teachers in grades six and eight reviewed and incorporated the proposed benchmarks for their respective grade levels into their teaching plans. They also received training in developing assessments related to benchmarks for their grade and subject area(s). Staff members trained by McREL facilitated this process during the first year of the grant.

THE THIRD YEAR AND BEYOND

During the third year (1998–99), teachers in grades six through eight were given the task of implementing the standards, benchmarks, and assessments in their instructional program. Teachers in grades three through five began the development of assessments to measure the standards and benchmarks identified the previous year. Finally, teachers in grades kindergarten through two began the development of standards and benchmarks for their grades. This last activity went so well that the standards and benchmarks were agreed upon before the end of the first semester. Members of the cross-district teams are in the process of showing members of their respective grade-level teams how to give all teachers the essential information they need to work with the standards, benchmarks, and assessments. This work is also designed to increase ownership by assisting each teacher with the task of planning lessons using the new system.

The curriculum teams now oversee the implementation of the standards and assessment at the district level and review test results to recommend necessary curriculum and instruction improvement efforts. By year five, each school guided its own improvement process and provided the district with diagnostic profiles derived from standards data. The evolving assessment system provided the information needed to monitor and guide change policies and practices.

The development, maintenance, and expansion of a technology infrastructure were crucial to the standards process. Concurrent with standards development, a consortium committee of technology specialists is working to develop student technology expectations and applications to be included in the standards and benchmarks for each subject area. Along with student performance, the technology committee is working to put in place software and hardware systems to aid in recording and reporting on assessment results and to facilitate teacher access to the standards-based lessons, units, and assessments. The committee is also designing training programs for teachers. By year five, staff development programs will include technology application components for both teachers and students.

STANDARD SPECIFICATIONS

Initially when laying out its project development plan, the consortium was plagued by two critical questions. The first question was how to sift through the vast array of standards documents that were flooding the national scene. Adding to the complexity were issues of levels of specificity and formatting. Each document had a different way of defining and organizing its standards. The answer for this question came from using the McREL database. McREL has translated the information from 85 different standards documents into one common format. Organized into traditional subject areas, the database made its task of standards definition and selection much easier.

The second question related to what kind of standards to adopt. This was not an easy question to deal with because of the multiplicity of approaches presented by different organizations and public entities with varying points of view toward standards development. In dealing with this dilemma, the consortium decided to keep it simple by organizing the standards around the traditional subject areas of language arts, mathematics, science, and social studies. Next, the definitions were sorted out to distinguish between types of standards. For system purposes, a standard served as a general category to organize knowledge within a subject area and/or to describe what a student should know or be able to do.

McREL helped us by providing three broad categories for standards:

1. Content standards, for what students should know and be able to do in a specific subject area
2. Lifelong learning standards, for what information and skills are applicable across all subject areas and connect closely to success in the workplace
3. Performance standards, for what constitutes qualitative levels for student performance as related to attainment of content standards

In year one, content standards were the first order of business for the consortium curriculum committees. The committees created incremental benchmarks to define a hierarchy of information and skills necessary at developmentally appropriate levels for each chosen standard. For example, one of its science standards reads: "Understands energy types, sources, and conversions, and their relationship to heat and temperature." Related benchmarks include:

- Grade 1: Knows that things that give off light often give off heat.
- Grade 3: Knows that an energy source, like a battery within a circuit, can produce light, sound, and heat.
- Grade 5: Knows that when warmer things are put with cooler ones, the warm ones lose heat and the cooler ones gain it until they are the same temperature.
- Grade 7: Understands that whenever the amount of energy in one place or form diminishes, the amount in other places or forms increases by the same amount.

Curriculum consistency and coherence is built in at the benchmark level. Benchmarks serve as the focal point for assessment design and for documenting progress toward standards. Developing content standards is only the first step. Lifelong learning standards are the next step in the process. Connecting content benchmarks with lifelong learning standards is essential for both planning instructional activities and designing or choosing assessments to measure student academic progress.

The importance of lifelong learning standards was accentuated in the SCANS report on what skills were needed to be productive members in the workplace. The scope of the lifelong learning standards includes skill categories such as complex thinking, information processing, communication, collaboration, cooperation, and habits of the mind. After drafting content standards and benchmarks, the task shifts to meaningful infusion of lifelong learning standards into content contexts. The intent is for lifelong learning skills to accent and enhance the learning and application of content standards and benchmarks.

Thus, during the second year, the consortium committees are learning this integration process by developing assessment and unit templates for use in future staff training.

Integrating content and lifelong learning standards into curriculum/assessment templates or prep sheets is demonstrated by the following example. This example connects mathematics content with three complex reasoning strategies. It demonstrates different possibilities for infusing complex reasoning strategies into content teaching. Templates such as this one will be used by teachers as a basis for classroom action research and in collaborative training and planning sessions.

Content Standard

"Understands and applies probability concepts to content benchmarks"

"Understands that probabilities are ratios that can be expressed as fractions, percentages, or odds"

"Uses mathematical/theoretical methods (for example, sample space, list, counting procedure, area model) to determine probabilities"

Task Scenario

Sometimes Mr. Stacy collects math homework assignments; sometimes he doesn't. When he collects homework, sometimes he grades it, and sometimes he just checks for completion. Mr. Stacy has a specific method for determining when he collects homework and which ones he will grade. He has not shared this process with the class. Your assignment record shows that for the first semester, out of 57 assignments, Mr. Stacy collected 42 and graded 34.

Complex Reasoning Strategies

Error Analysis: Your friend asks to you to go to the football game after school. You say that you can't because you have homework for Mr. Stacy. Your friend tells you not to sweat it because there is only a 50-50 chance that Mr. Stacy will collect the homework and the odds are even less that he'll grade it. Explain to your friend what you think about his argument.

Abstracting: Using information about Mr. Stacy's homework collection method and your knowledge about theoretical probability, explain how you think his homework and grading system works. Describe the general pattern of this situation and identify instances in another subject area where you find the same pattern.

Deduction: You have homework due in Mr. Stacy's class, but you also don't want to miss your favorite shows on TV. Analyzing Mr. Stacy's homework collection and grading system, what can you conclude about the probability that he will collect your homework tomorrow? That he will actually grade it? The identification and implementation of area-wide content and lifelong learning standards are the first steps for increasing the consistency and intentionality of instructional decision making in each building, in each district, and across the whole consortium. Assessment is another critical step.

Establishing performance standards is critical to assessment reform. In the past, assessment has been a major barrier to system reform. First, system-wide assessment programs relied on normative data to provide feedback for program improvement planning. Criterion-referenced data were unreliable because there was a lack of uniform criteria across classroom, grade level, building, and district lines for analysis purposes. Next, assessment techniques were mainly content-based, failing to provide needed data on student use and mastery of higher-level skills that characterized the lifelong learning standards. Lastly, assessment instruments lacked clear sets of criteria for the learner as to what constituted different levels of proficiency. Reliable and valid ways were needed to provide methods to measure student progress toward achieving the chosen standards.

The main goal is to develop an assessment system that relies heavily on classroom teachers to assess students on standards and benchmarks. Teachers need to be trained in developing their own assessment tools and be given alternative assessment instruments to be used in classrooms. Types of assessment instruments include:

- Tests provided by the Wisconsin Student Assessment System (WSAS) at grades four, eight, and ten
- Selected-response grade-level unit tests developed by the consortium committees for each subject area
- Grade-level performance tasks with clearly defined rubrics for each subject area
- The use of student performance portfolios where students can select work products to meet specified performance criteria

Again McREL is needed to help in designing an assessment system. McREL will provide training and technical advice at each step of this development process. The process of analyzing to determine which McREL benchmarks are to be adopted is being assessed through instruments already in place. This study includes looking to determine which of the benchmarks are covered by the current state testing program. Along with state tests, the school is analyzing different district tests to determine which ones can best be used at the consortium level. The key factor in the analysis is correlation with the content benchmarks and life-long learning standards. Once it was determined which benchmarks and standards are not included in current, valid, and reliable assessments, then it was necessary to determine how many and what kind of assessment tools were needed or needed to be developed.

PROFESSIONAL DEVELOPMENT

Staff development activities are at the heart of this project. McREL provided initial training to the teams at the consortium level. Individuals on cross-district curriculum teams were trained to facilitate staff development at the district and building levels. Staff training needs depended on which level individuals are serving—consortium, district, or building. At the consortium level, professional development activities emphasized training in the Dimensions of Learning model to set a foundation for determining standards, designing assessments, and planning instructional strategies. People trained included members of the area coordinating committee and cross-district curriculum teams. The training included:

- Developing an understanding of content and lifelong learning standards
- Understanding the five dimensions of learning
- Applying Dimensions of Learning as a decision-making model for determining standards/benchmarks, designing assessments, and planning lessons/units
- Distinguishing between alternative, genuine, and performance assessments
- Designing reliable, valid assessments to measure student progress in meeting identified standards
- Developing presentation/team-building skills for training staff members in local districts

The Dimensions of Learning framework, which provides for students developing positive attitudes toward learning, acquiring, and using knowledge meaningfully and developing productive mind habits, serves as the basis for building the standards-based program. McREL and trained regional Dimensions of Learning specialists will provide the initial training in the use of this model. At the district level, training includes members of the district curriculum and subject area curriculum teams.

District staff trained at the consortium level (with technical consultation by McREL) provided training. Training sessions emphasized:

- Developing an understanding of content and lifelong learning standards
- Understanding the five Dimensions of Learning
- Learning how to incorporate multiple intelligence theory into Dimensions of Learning planning
- Establishing benchmarks at designated grade levels to meet district standards
- Integrating standards/benchmarks and assessments into instructional planning
- Understanding and using rubrics for scoring and reporting student performance
- Learning pilot procedures for the new standards and assessments
- Learning presentation and team building strategies for working with staff

Participants are being trained to pilot the standards and assessment programs at the eighth-grade level. Participants are learning how to integrate alternative assessment strategies into their instructional planning effectively. Here the Dimensions of Learning model is expanded to include knowledge and strategies for multiple intelligence. The intent is to increase student engagement and achievement for various student subgroups (for example, female and minority student achievement in science and mathematics). The successes and mistakes at this level guide implementation strategies for developing benchmarks and assessments at other grade levels.

At the individual building level, district subject area curriculum team members (with support from the area representatives from their district) train staff members. The training sessions focus on learning the Dimensions of Learning framework, developing benchmarks, administering/ scoring/interpreting assessments, and planning units based on a Dimensions of Learning and multiple intelligence framework. Building-level training includes:

- Developing an understanding of content and lifelong learning standards
- Understanding the five Dimensions of Learning
- Learning how to incorporate multiple intelligence into Dimensions of Learning planning
- Establishing benchmarks at designated grade levels to meet district standards

- Integrating standards/benchmarks and assessments into instructional planning
- Understanding and using rubrics for scoring and reporting student performance
- Learning how to work collaboratively to implement the standards and assessment program

The emphasis for all training sessions uses instructional strategies that create continuous, interdependent linkages between instruction and assessment. Valid and reliable assessments will stand as the basis for school improvement decisions.

CONCLUSION

Many steps have been necessary to build an assessment-driven curriculum where achievement of district content and lifelong learning standards is measurable and connected to producing complex thinkers and quality producers. The schools have a long way to go before everything is in place. The process of implementing a standards-based instructional program is by itself one of continual improvement. Each step along the way will reveal new and better ways of doing things.

To improve student learning, a district must be results oriented. There must be a process in place that focuses on student performance, that generates appropriate data about this performance, and that uses these data to plan for continual improvement. The school districts comprising the Nicolet area believe that the standards project as described in this article will accomplish this goal. Doing so requires, and will continue to require, leadership, the empowerment of a committed staff, and the cooperation of all those who have a stake in the success of its school districts. It is hoped that the process and results obtained become a model for other districts as they continue their journey of continuous improvement.

ABOUT THE AUTHOR

Robert Kattman was the Superintendent of the Glendale-River Hills Schools in Milwaukee, Wisconsin, for 28 years. He serves as the ASQ Education Division's Immediate Past Chair and has been its Vice-Chair for K–12 Schools. Currently he is the Director for Charter Schools at the University of Wisconsin-Milwaukee.

REFERENCES

Dolan, W. Patrick. *Restructuring Its Schools—A Primer on Systemic Change.* Kansas City, MO: Systems and Organizations, 1994.

Gomes, Hélio. *Quality Quotes.* Milwaukee: ASQ Quality Press, 1996.

Malcolm Baldrige National Quality Award Criteria for Performance Excellence. Milwaukee: American Society for Quality, 1999.

Malcolm Baldrige National Quality Award Pilot Program. Milwaukee: American Society for Quality, 1995.

Marzano, Robert J. and John S. Kendall. *Designing Standards-Based Districts, Schools, and Classrooms.* Alexandria, VA: Association for Supervision and Curriculum Development and Oxford, OH: National Staff Development Council, 1996.

The Secretary's Commission on Achieving Necessary Skills. *What Work Requires of Schools: A SCANS Report for America 2000.* Washington, D.C.: U.S. Department of Labor, 1991.

Sparks, Dennis and Stephanie Hirsh. *A New Vision for Staff Development.* Alexandria, VA: Association for Supervision and Curriculum Development and Oxford, OH: National Staff Development Council, 1997.

7

Continual Improvement

Grant Smith

INTRODUCTION

All schools test students continually to be sure their learning is improving. Support services continue to find new ways to improve food service, transportation, and maintenance. These are valuable activities and should continue in all schools. However, schools with immature quality management systems may encounter two kinds of problems as they continually attempt to improve. First, some improvements may cancel other improvements. For example, enabling teachers to set their own work schedules may diminish the ability of teams to schedule meetings. Second, the improvement may treat symptoms of a problem and delay eliminating the root cause that continues to create more problems.

To avoid these negative effects, schools with a mature quality system take corrective or preventive action to avoid improvements that cancel each other out and direct their improvement effort toward root causes. This often requires root cause analysis based on a combination of data and intuition. Root cause is seldom obvious even in a mature quality system. An example from a local K–12 school was found in an unpublished investigation conducted by Robert Gagne.

Professor Gagne was interested in the question, "What do K–12 students think about when they get consistently wrong answers on math tests?" He discovered that these students worked as hard and spent the same amount of time on problems as students who consistently got the right answers. He observed and interviewed 30 such students and found

> *many who did not read the question properly, some who did not know how to answer the kind of questions asked, and others who applied computational rules incorrectly. One student, for example, consistently applied a rule that said, "Given two numbers in a column, when the top number is larger then subtract; when the top number is smaller then add." When this wrong rule was applied to the student's latest failing paper, he scored 100 percent. The root cause had been found. When the student applied the right rule, the improvement was total and permanent.*

Effective corrective and preventive action often focuses on the process. Improving input often lies outside the control of the school. Lester Maddox, while governor of Georgia, said, "We could improve our prisons if they sent us a better class of prisoners." Raising output goals without changing the process almost never improves the result.

CONTINUAL PROCESS IMPROVEMENT
IN SCHOOL DISTRICTS

Improvement begins with reliable measures. Two examples of measures used for continual improvement based on root cause analysis come from the Schoolyear 2000 project in the Florida Public Schools. In the first example, seven school districts identified processes that were unwieldy, sometimes outdated, and often inefficient. The purpose was, in part, to improve these selected processes and this purpose was accomplished. The second purpose was to give the administrators and staff experience in using quality tools to improve processes.

In the second example, an alternative school agreed to do an in-depth study for the root causes of ineffective behavior modification processes. The purpose was to identify the major root cause and this purpose was accomplished. The second purpose was to demonstrate that processes in schools could be used to establish the stability and capability of processes as a necessary prerequisite for continual improvement. As Deming points out, changes made to processes that are not stable and capable is "tinkering" and wastes resources.

IMPROVEMENT IN SCHOOLS

The seven projects reported here established a baseline for continual improvement. They demonstrated the feasibility of providing basic quality tools to staff and administrators to achieve results in the form of improved processes and quality savings. The following conditions were adhered to for each project.

- **Build on Success.** Team members were asked to select a process that was clearly in need of improvement. The reason for this was that a successful demonstration in an obvious case would motivate the staff and administrators to identify other processes in need of improvement. A caution was added to these conditions. Be sure that you are not merely attacking symptoms without a clear idea of possible root causes. This will prevent the false security of eliminating symptoms while the root causes continue to generate problem elsewhere in the system.

- **Target 20 percent savings.** The purpose was not to set a numerical goal, but rather to specify in advance the kind of saving intended. The improvements could be documented by savings of time, money, number of steps in a process, and so on.

- **Describe the relationships.** Flowcharts are a nonstatistical way to describe the relationships among steps in a process. Once these relationships are described, obvious inconsistencies, gaps, or needed additions become apparent. The improvement is then based in objective reality.

- **Follow established guidelines for process improvement.** Many such guidelines are available in the quality literature. These have been successfully applied in many fields and were easily adapted to processes in schools. The specific guidelines selected by the seven school districts were the following:
  - **Select a process.** Each of the seven school districts selected a process based on the guidelines above. The processes selected were grade reports, attendance zone variance, absentee monitoring, exceptional children referrals, psycho-education referrals, employment applications, and Section 540 procedures for exceptional children.
  - **Flowchart the process.** One member from each district attended a one-day workshop. A brief set of instructions were provided including options of manual and software flowcharting techniques. Each district member then flowcharted the process selected by the district. The flowcharts were then evaluated by the group and suggestions were made for process improvement and quality savings.
  - **Change the process and measure improvements.** This step was taken when the seven district representatives returned to their respective districts. No two districts followed the same procedure for their measurement and analysis. In some cases, the process changes needed to be revised several times and tested again. Eventually all seven districts achieved success.
  - **Report the savings.** The reports not only described the methods and findings but also suggested additional processes that

were likely to benefit from systematic process improvement. Having examples of school improvement to share with stakeholders proved to be advantageous to the district when dealing with them.

PROCESS IMPROVEMENT RESULTS

Small School Districts (Number of students)

Dixie County (2227) examined the psycho-educational evaluation process because of the high cost—two to three times that of students in regular classrooms. In addition, each evaluation cost the school $250. A review of the flowchart revealed that all students were subjected to a battery of 10 tests before presenting possible candidates for the special classroom to the school psychologist. This process was replaced by a plan-do-check-act for a sequence of testing from easier interventions to those that are more difficult. This process reduced the annual cost of referrals by $20,000.

Madison County (3359) selected the referral process for exceptional children. The quality team leader selected this process because the district reviewed 300 referrals each year. Improvement of this process was of interest to parents who were concerned about the length of time between the referral and the meeting with the parents to discuss the results. Many phone calls were received from anxious parents. The steps in the flowchart were reviewed and 20 minutes were eliminated from each of the 300 reviews. This resulted in cost savings of $3132 each year and provided earlier notification to parents.

Levy County (5450) undertook the task of revising the absence monitoring process. This was judged to be a complex problem and of great concern to the district's Principal's Committee. Using a combination of computer-based technology for communication purposes, the original 20-step process was reduced to 10, eliminating petitioning committee meetings and reducing the number of mailings from eight to three with no loss in effectiveness. There were time savings and reduced workloads for each assistant principal and attendance clerk, and department chairs were saved from having to attend petitioning committee meetings.

Medium-Sized Districts

Santa Rosa County (18,972) applied quality tools to Section 504 of a federally mandated law for students with disabilities. Initial cost estimates for implementing this new law included the addition of one full-time staff member. Flowcharts were prepared for both the existing procedures and for the procedures under the new law. These flowcharts were reviewed by a team of district personnel and school administrators. The result of the review was that the new law was implemented with no new costs to the school district.

Pasco County (40,114) had a process for filling vacant positions that involved one-fifth of the time of the Supervisor of Personnel. An examination of the flowchart determined that time-consuming tasks in the process were clerical in nature and could be accomplished by a level 2 Personnel Assistant. In addition to a savings of $7600 in salary costs, the new procedures made the selection process for filling vacant positions more effective.

Volusia County (55,530) found that the zone school variance application process affected many special processes for psychological, physical handicaps, medical, curriculum, employment, racial balance, and administrative variances. The flowchart analysis suggested two ways to improve each process by type of variance and improved the process for determining zone school variance request proposals. This resulted in an annual savings of $23,000 in personnel costs.

Large-Sized District

Orange County (118,666) selected the grade reporting process for middle and high schools. The quality team began by clarifying the process based on the initial flowchart. The original process generated approximately 800 reports every nine weeks. On average, each report was 50 pages long and took two minutes to print. By making two changes in the process, the quality review team was able to save 35,000 sheets of paper ($532 annually) and 24 hours of computer time (48 personnel-hours, $2600 annually). Due to this success, the district applied quality review to student attendance processes as well.

These first steps in the continual improvement objective were done by people who understood the administrative system within each school district. The results, though significant, were for specific problems with an immediate objective of learning how to flowchart processes and to reduce needless spending of resources. The search for root causes is often a more formal, complex, and time-consuming effort as illustrated in the case study.

PROCESS IMPROVEMENT

An early childhood memory, for many people, is of a teacher who said, "Class! May I have your attention, please?" The teacher said this to let students know it was time to begin working. In today's public schools, this verbal command has not been enough for about 10 percent of the students. They have been diagnosed as having an attention deficit disorder, a condition that has made it difficult for them to maintain their attention span. Overcoming this problem requires a combination of trained teachers, smaller classrooms, alternative schools, prescribed medication, and federal funds. Alternative public schools have employed teachers trained to observe students, to record students' off-task behavior, to analyze the recorded data, and to find appropriate interventions to modify the behavior.

These students with behavior problems provided a special opportunity for Florida's educational reform initiative Schoolyear 2000 (SY2000). Its vision states, "Each student shall acquire the basic skills and competencies needed to succeed in the information age." This vision included attention deficit students who need to control their learning behavior.

The Riverview Learning Center is one of the 44 Florida public schools which had been designated as a test site for SY2000. Riverview is an alternative school that enrolls attention deficit students who have been referred by qualified medical, legal, or educational professionals.

THE PURPOSE

The purpose of the case study was to determine what a process capability study could contribute to the continuous improvement of learning processes.

THE SETTING

Riverview began each school year with an enrollment of approximately 50 students. Upon enrolling, each student was placed into a group. This group remained together throughout the day as it moved from class to class. During the year, new students transferred in to Riverview, some students left Riverview after successfully completing their instruction, while other students left Riverview without completing their instruction. This student migration caused the number of students to rise above or to fall below 50 on any given day.

There were six full-time teachers in addition to an administrative staff. The goal of each teacher was to provide timely and effective intervention to modify a student's behavior until the student was able to attend to schoolwork well enough to return to the school from which he or she had been referred. The teachers observed each student three times during each class period and recorded measurements indicating whether the student was on-task or off-task. Each student was measured 18 times each day for a five-week period.

THE SAMPLE

To accomplish the purpose, Riverview's average of 50 students was divided into rational subgroups (for a discussion of rational subgroups see Shewhart, 1931). Rational subgroups of data contained 18 individual measures on 50 students per day over 65 days for a total sample size of 58,500 individual student measures.

THE METHOD

The process capability study method was an initial step toward applying process control to learning in public schools. The study assumed the degree of attention paid to the learning process varied between on-task learning behavior and off-task learning behavior while an individual student attended Riverview. Process capability was evaluated by comparing teachers' observations of task behavior with the five advancement requirements.

Process stability was established by examining the data distribution or randomness. When the learning process displayed only random variation, the process was stable and predictable. For example, if a student was on-task more than 80 percent of the day for a number of days, the learning task behavior was in control. However, if a second student was on-task 100 percent for the same number of days, followed by one day when the student was on-task less than 80 percent of the time, the learning process was out of control because one unusual measurement made the process unpredictable.

QUALITY TOPICS

Over the year and one-half devoted to this case study, many quality topics related to process capability and stability were introduced, discussed, and acted upon while Riverview continued its daily operation. These quality topics included the following:

- A customer driven system
- Special processes
- The plan-do-check-act cycle
- Control charts

- Conformity measures for behavior specification
- Collecting and coding data
- Special causes
- Interpretation of student performance data by teachers and students

MAJOR EVENTS

The following summary is provided to document how discussions and activities carried out during the case study were viewed, related to quality topics, and resolved. For example, absence was a special cause, evaluation of on-task behavior after the student was returned to the referring school was a special process, and the teacher's intervention was part of the plan-do-check-act cycle. The transition from a discussion to a problem resolution evolved over time.

In June of 1994, Riverview approached SY2000 regarding possible technology to improve its process for increasing a student's attention span. An agreement was made to test a pen-based computer for recording observations of students and to conduct a process capability study to analyze students' on-task learning behavior. The case study presented here covers the process capability study and not the use of the pen-based computer.

A staff member from SY2000 was assigned responsibility for conducting the process capability study. During the next two months, several visits were made to Riverview and the following steps were taken:

- A measurement scale was defined as dichotomous variables with a binomial distribution
- A literature review was made of p/np charts and properties of binomial distributions
- A library search on control charts was conducted which yielded few references
- A data collection and analysis program was selected

During the fall of 1994, a team was formed which included the SY2000 staff member, Riverview's assistant principal, and a classroom teacher. The purpose of the first team meeting was to acquaint the SY2000 staff member with Riverview's behavior modification process, which included the following:

- Individual student's records—carried by each student to all classes
- Teachers' data entries—every 20 minutes, 18 times per day
- Student's behavior criteria—a student appeared engaged in an assigned task

- Teacher training—workshops where the on-task criteria were explained and discussed
- Baseline data—established from control charts from a sample of 1993 students' records
- Staff verification—of baseline control charts

The Riverview goals for the process capability study were to reduce off-task behavior, to increase task completion, and to increase attendance. The goals were accomplished by a five-step progression plan with measurable minimum specifications at each step. The specifications were derived from the daily task measures. Each step required increasingly greater effort from the student. The program was completed when a student successfully completed each of the five steps.

During several meetings with the Riverview staff, control charts were proposed as a way to improve the teachers' rating process because the charts provided a visual display, synthesized information, and reduced the time required to determine the appropriate intervention. The expectation was that control charts would help students to review their own behavior and assist them in controlling it. The baseline data from the previous year were used to familiarize teachers with control charts, interpretation of control limits, centerlines, out-of-control points, and the advantages of process stability.

In the winter of 1994, the final version of data entry software was loaded onto a Riverview base workstation. Student data from 1993 were used to demonstrate how the data on individual students, student groups, and students grouped by teacher schedule would be displayed. The data collection for the process capability study was scheduled to begin in January 1995 at the start of Riverview's second semester. The data were to be transferred between Quattro Pro, Access, and Quality Analyst software programs.

This was not the ideal way to process the data. It was as slow and labor intensive as it was practical for the limited purpose of this process capability study. A faster and less labor-intensive way would have included coded behavior scales scanned by teachers using a laser pen.

At the January 20 meeting, the team reviewed the enrollment, student schedules, and teacher assignments, which had been provided in December. This review necessitated modifications to the data input program. Data were collected and entered for the first week of the 1995 school year.

For the remainder of the winter of 1995, the SY2000 staff member collected the student folders each week, entered the data into the appropriate computer programs, created control charts, and reviewed the charts with the Riverview staff. This process resulted in discussions among the team about the purpose, process, and results of behavior modification at Riverview.

In the middle of February 1995, the team discussed student's folders. Some folders had data missing. The Riverview staff members explained that a student not in attendance should have been recorded on the folder as being absent. However, when the folder was blank for a given day Riverview assumed the student was absent. This became important in March when inferences were made about on-task or off-task behavior for absent students.

In the middle of March 1995, the SY2000 staff member reviewed with the Riverview staff a set of student control charts which showed the behavior modification process was out of control for most students. Absences appeared to contribute the largest proportion of the variance.

A Pareto chart on a sample of students revealed over 95 percent of off-task measures were due to absences. The Riverview staff suggested absences should be removed from the process capability study.

Riverview's goals and the procedures for a capability study were reviewed to determine if this deletion of data was appropriate. While no one contended that absence was on-task behavior, there was some discussion as to whether or not excused absence should be counted as out of control behavior. The SY2000 staff member was asked to present the implication for the analysis when absences were removed from the data.

During this time period, the interest in the capability study appeared to increase when Riverview's data were displayed in a control chart form. The staff suggested posting control charts in classrooms so each group could compare its performance with other groups in each teacher's class. Various charts were presented. There was a limited discussion of control chart concepts and possible interventions.

In several meetings, the SY2000 staff member prepared control charts for a discussion of the relationship between process stability and process capability. It was noted that Riverview was operating under a specifications-based system for quality control. The current specifications were compared to simulated distributions of student measurements to show that the existing specifications did not mandate students be in statistical control to successfully complete a step. Other simulated distributions showed that students under statistical control would fail to meet the minimum specifications for success although their daily task behavior was superior.

The Riverview staff said they were aware of this but were unsure how to address it. During this discussion, concern was expressed about the term "out of control." The staff wanted to know what was causing the "out of control" condition. Pareto chart results were presented which listed absenteeism as the primary cause. Riverview staff wanted to know what changes could be made to gain control. Strategies were considered to reduce absenteeism, to adjust the measurement scale, and to revisit the goals. The SY2000 staff member agreed to prepare control charts to illustrate the impact of an adjusted measurement scale.

The following week, the SY2000 staff member presented the control charts, which illustrated the impact of an adjusted measurement scale. This included alternative methods for, or discriminating between, excused and unexcused absences with a different weight given to each. Following this discussion, the Riverview staff determined that absences were not part of the behavior modification process and should not be included. The scale, adjusted from a two-point to a four-point scale, was well received and was adopted for a trial in the upcoming summer term.

In the spring of 1995, the SY2000 staff member consulted with a statistician on the measurement scale adjustments and the recording of absences. The discussion centered on semi-variables from the Western Electric handbook. The statistician concluded that plotting ratings on an X-bar chart was a reasonable strategy using a second chart to monitor absences in a bivariate process.

During this time, there was an unexpectedly large enrollment increase at Riverview and the decision was made to divide the students between the high school and middle school. Three teachers were added. It was agreed that the process capability study would limit data collection to the middle school. Control charts, with absences removed, were presented and discussed. Many students were still out of control due to lack of variability. The two-point measurement scale and a small number of observations within the subgroups contributed to the inability to detect variability. Informal discussion with teachers suggested the measurement process as a potential cause of the lack of variability. Further, teachers had intervened to bring an off-task student back on-task and noted the behavior only after the intervention. Pre-intervention measurements were not taken because it was not part of the progress plan procedures.

At subsequent meetings, the measurement process was discussed with the SY2000 staff member, as was the practice of training teachers to intervene before measuring. Uncertainty remained regarding when the measures were recorded. The Riverview staff agreed to test the adjusted rating scale in the high school for the summer term and the SY2000 staff member provided the training. The high school teachers agreed to measure before an intervention.

In the summer term of 1995, the Riverview High School teachers taught for more than two weeks without using rating scales while they were adjusting to their new assignments. Despite the sincere intention to use the adjusted rating, they decided not to do so until the following year after the three new teachers were more accustomed to their teaching assignment. Data continued to be collected, control charts were prepared and reviewed by teachers, and issues associated with control charts were discussed.

At the end of the summer of 1995, the process capability study was completed. The technical details of the process capability study, sample control charts, and recommendations for action at Riverview based on the results of the study are presented below.

THE SPECIFICATIONS

Riverview converted into specified limits the existing criteria associated with the successful completion of the five required steps. The limits were set in terms of off-task behavior, which was the measure plotted on control charts.

Control charts (for an example of a control chart see Figure 1.3, Student run chart) were used to access process capability and stability of the behavior modification process at Riverview. It was possible for a control chart to show a process which was in control (stable) and yet not capable. Process capability was not estimated for unstable processes. The upper and lower limits of the control charts were calculated based on an estimate of the average value for the entire distribution and an estimate of the average variability of the distribution. Roughly, the control limits are calculated with a formula similar to:

$$\text{UCL/LCL} = [(\text{average off-task}) +/-3 \times (\text{average variability})]$$

Theoretically, approximately 99 percent of all measurements should have fallen within these limits for a process to be predictable. When the control chart indicated measures exceeding the control limits, the process was out of control and unpredictable. Process capability was estimated using a formula selected from among a variety of accepted formulas, which required established specification limits compared with estimated process variability.

Essentially, it was a ratio of "acceptable" variability/observed variability. Values equal to or greater than one indicated that the process was capable since the observed variability did not exceed the "acceptable" variability. Values less than one indicated that the process was not capable of producing output within the specification limits 100 percent of the time.

The Riverview system of student task behavior operationalized the task behaviors required for successful completion of each of the five steps in the program. These conditions provide a method for defining the upper and lower specification limits required to estimate process capability.

THE MEASUREMENT

The measurements taken at Riverview at the end of the mandatory time period for each step compared students' task behavior with required behavior. Process capability measures were also taken at the end of each mandatory time period. It was assumed that the students who were evaluated three times per hour were encouraged to stay on-task.

Since process capability measures were taken at the end of each of five two-week periods, it was not possible to collect daily process capability measures. The Riverview measurement system allowed students who met the minimum step completion criteria to advance without maintaining process stability.

THE DATA

There were over 600 control charts prepared for this case study and reviewed by the Riverview staff and teachers. The overall control chart for Riverview during the 77 days of this study summarizes over 63,000 individual measurements on 50 students recorded by six teachers. There were 55 out-of-control points. Absences accounted for 80 percent of the variability. When absence was removed from the data, the school remained out of statistical control.

The following summary tables taken from a sample of eight (#12, 93, 40, 02, 33, 82, 37, 90) individual student's control chart results provided examples of the how these data are used to form conclusions about the student's performance. Two (#12 and #92) of these student's charts illustrate the process (see Figures 7.1 and 7.2).

Interpretation: The learning process for student #12 was stable. The student successfully met the Riverview specifications for step 5. There was no variability in the process. This is an example of a stable and capable process that can be improved. Table 7.1 summarizes the control chart data into a user-friendly format for classroom teachers.

Interpretation: The learning process for student #93 was not stable. This student successfully met the requirements for step 3 but did not meet the 82 percent compliance requirement for step 4. While the assessment at step 3 indicated the ability to go on to step 4, the indication was that off-task behavior needed to be investigated before the process was capable and could be improved. Table 7.2 summarizes these data.

Table 7.3 presents the summary data for all eight students in the sample to illustrate what the classroom teachers used to guide the student's activities to encourage more on-task behavior.

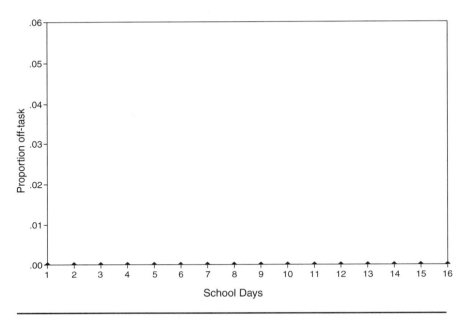

Figure 7.1 Summary of off-task measures for student #12.

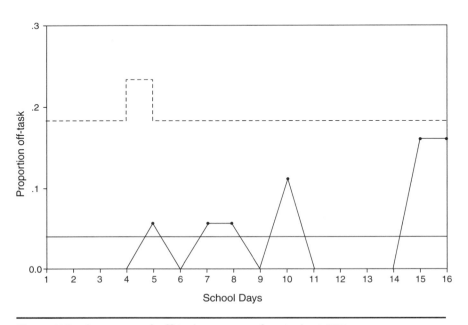

Figure 7.2 Summary of off-task measures for student #93.

Table 7.1 Data for student #12.

Chart 1 Student #12		Stable	Capable for Steps 1-3	Capable for Steps 1-4	Capable for Steps 1-5	Absences
1	12	Yes			Yes	Included

Table 7.2 Data for student #93.

Chart 2 Student #93		Stable	Capable for Steps 1-3	Capable for Steps 1-4	Capable for Steps 1-5	Absences
2	93	No	Yes			Included

Table 7.3 Control chart data for all eight students in the sample.

Chart 3 Student #		Stable	Capable for Steps 1-3	Capable for Steps 1-4	Capable for Steps 1-5	Absences
1	12	Yes			Yes	Included
2	93	No	Yes			Included
3	49	No		Yes		Included
4	02	No		Yes		Included
5	02	No				Excluded
6	33	No		Yes		Included
7	33	No		Yes		Excluded
8	82	No				Included
9	82	Yes				Excluded
10	37	No		Yes		Included
11	37	No		Yes		Excluded
12	90	No				Included
13	90	Yes			Yes	Excluded

Summary of Data

The major characteristics that needed process improvement were:

1. Absence from the task was the major special cause
2. Insensitive measures of on-task behavior when absence was removed
3. Inconsistent measurement process due to inaccurate absence records

The most typical behavior patterns were, in order of frequency:

1. In control and at an appropriate progress rate
2. Out of control when absent and in control when in attendance
3. Stable but not capable
4. Stable and capable

The progress rates in order of frequency:

1. Decreased in variability over time
2. No change over time
3. Increasing variability over time

CONCLUSIONS AND PROCESS IMPROVEMENTS

The conclusions and recommendations are related to the quality topic.

- *A customer driven system*—Prior to the case study, Riverview developed its specifications within the school. Following the case study, Riverview consulted extensively with the principals of the referring schools.
- *Special processes*—Prior to the case study, Riverview measured student on-task behavior until the progress plan was completed. After the case study, Riverview visited the referring school to see if the students were able to maintain on-task behavior in a regular classroom.
- *The plan-do-check-act cycle*—Prior to the case study, Riverview followed a plan-do-act-check cycle. After the case study, Riverview's followed a plan-do-check-act cycle.
- *Control charts*—Prior to the case study, the Riverview bivariate grading system was restricted to p/np charts. After the case study, Riverview used a 4-point grading system and an X-bar chart.
- *Conformity measures for behavior specification*—Prior to the case study, Riverview measured disruptive and non-disruptive behavior and collected no data on cause. After the case study, Riverview collected conformity data and possible causes which enabled Pareto analyses.
- *Collecting and coding data*—Prior to the case study, Riverview was interested in a $3000 pen-based computer system for each teacher. After the case study, Riverview was interested in a light pen and laser system, which would cost less than $500 per teacher.
- *Special causes*—Before the case study, Riverview was unaware of absences as the major cause of process instability. After the case

study, Riverview treated the absence problem as a separate process and began to study and improve the process.

* *Interpretation of student performance data by teachers and students—* Prior to the case study, Riverview made no effort to show students how they could use data to control their own learning behavior. After the case study, trends and possible causes of off-task behavior were discussed with students based on the control charts.

ABOUT THE AUTHOR

Grant Smith, a former K–12 teacher, conducted the research in this chapter as a doctoral student in Educational Research. He is currently an analyst working on contracts for Johnson & Johnson specializing in surgical devices. He works almost exclusively on the design and analysis of two types of studies: business case forecasting and product design.

REFERENCES

Cheng, Smiley W. "Practical Implementation of the Process Capability Indices." *Quality Engineering* 7 (1995): 239–259.

DeVor, Richard E., Tsong-how Chang, and John W. Sutherland. *Statistical Quality Design and Control,* New York: Macmillan Publishing Co., 1992.

Melvin, Charles A. "Application of Control Charts to an Educational System." *Performance Improvement Quarterly* 6 (July 1994): 74–85.

Rodriguez, Robert N. "Recent Developments in Process Capability Analysis." *Journal of Quality Technology* 24 (1992): 176–187.

Shewhart, Walter A. *Economic Control of Quality of Manufactured Product.* New York: D. Van Nostrand Co., 1931.

Western Electric Company. *AT&T Statistical Quality Control Handbook.* Easton, PA: Western Electric Company, 1956.

8

Systems in K–12 Schools

Frank Caplan

INTRODUCTION

How does an administrator know that a quality management system exists, perhaps under a different name, and how can administrators estimate the system's maturity? The complete answer is to have a quality professional look at the system and make an evaluation against a standard like ISO 9001 or make a relative judgment using the Baldrige criteria. This complete answer is most beneficial after a quality system is in place, and that often requires expenditure of substantial time and money.

Self-analysis is a less expensive way to answer these two questions. An example of a self-analysis method is presented in the first part of this chapter and provides a no-cost self-analysis that anyone thoroughly familiar with the school can complete in an hour or two dependent on the quality system's scope. If the scope involves one school, then the principal should be able to complete the self-analysis within an hour. If the scope is larger and involves one or more districts it may require several people and more time to complete the self-analysis.

The second part of this chapter presents an example of a quality management system with a large and complex scope that included all schools in Florida. The first stage of development for a quality management system is presented for the seven test sites and consisted of 119 interconnected learning and supporting processes. Each process was described and flowcharted. *All* of the seven districts adapted the design to accommodate their different curriculum objectives, different instructional methods, and different administrative practices, resulting in quality management systems that were tailored to individual conditions.

SELF-ASSESSMENT OF QUALITY SYSTEM MATURITY

Many models currently exist for a school to self-assess its quality management system. The most widely recognized and used one is the Baldrige excellence model. The intent of self-assessment is to provide fact-based guidance to the school regarding where to invest resources for improvement. The self-assessment methodology described in this chapter is generic and is intended to provide a general, simple, and easy-to-use approach to determine the relative degree of maturity of a school's quality management system and to identify areas for improvement.

Specific features of this self-assessment model are that it can be:

- Applied to the entire school or a part of the school
- Completed in a short period of time by one person who knows the details of all activities within the scope
- Completed by a small team if the scope includes several schools
- Used to guide the development of a more comprehensive quality management system
- Used to prioritize improvement opportunities
- Used to guide movement toward a world-class quality management system

The structure is designed to evaluate quality management system maturity on a scale ranging from 1 (no formal system) to 5 (best-in-class performance) and provides guidance in the form of typical questions that the school should ask to evaluate its system. Another advantage is that the results of the first use serves as a baseline for improvement progress.

System Maturity Levels

The performance maturity levels are shown in Table 8.1.

Self-Assessment Questions

The questions should be answered based on the amount of effort it would take to convince a person who is knowledgeable about quality management systems that a school's quality system meets the requirements of a standard or the criteria of a quality award. The assumption is that a school with a mature quality management system can produce convincing evidence of an effective system at any time. If a long period of time, requiring special effort, is required to collect the evidence, than the school's system is less mature. The following questions provide a general overview of what evidence a school should be able to provide at any time to demonstrate that it is operating according to the eight quality princi-

Table 8.1 Performance maturity levels.

Level	People involved	Expectation	Symptoms
1	None	Random changes and unknown results	No evidence of a systematic approach, no results, poor results, or unpredictable results
2	Few staff part time	Corrected results based on complaints	Anecdotal evidence of problem-correction approach, reduced complaints, individual results adjusted
3	Most staff for limited time periods	Corrective action on defective processes and future defects	Evidence of a process approach, occasional measurement, limited data available on meeting objectives, a corrective action system, and some routine self-assessment of effectiveness
4	All staff few faculty	Efficient academic system improvement	Records maintained on systems performance, routine self-assessment of efficiency, and verified learning and support improvement
5	All staff all faculty	Highest performance always improving	Records of a systems approach for all processes, valid results, optimum efficiency, preventive system maintenance, and innovation

ples. Detailed self-assessments are available from the Baldrige Education Criteria for Performance Excellence or from the standard ANSI/ASQC Z1.11-1996.

Student and Stakeholder

The quality management system should be designed to understand the needs, meet the requirements, and strive to exceed the expectations of all students and other stakeholders.

What evidence is there that the school has identified student and stakeholder needs and expectations on a regular basis? How does the school identify students' need for recognition, schoolwork satisfaction, competence, and development of knowledge? What evidence is there that stakeholder needs and expectations result in meeting long-term objectives? How does the school establish its requirements in accordance with the laws of society? How does the quality system lead to visible and expected improvements?

Learning and Supporting Processes

Quality system plans and objectives should provide clear focus on important support areas throughout the school and enhance learning in the classroom. What evidence is there that plans and objectives translate into measurable goals? How are the objectives deployed to each school level to assure individual contribution for achievement? What evidence is there that the quality management system ensures that processes are optimized to give predictable results at minimal costs? How does the quality management system communicate responsibilities for learning and supporting processes? What evidence is there that administrative review leads to optimal processes within the quality system?

Empowering People

The quality management system should be designed to give a better understanding of roles, responsibilities, and goals to enhance involvement of people at all levels in the school; to encourage recognition; and to reward the empowerment of people. What evidence is there that the school promotes understanding of employee's roles, responsibilities, and involvement? How does the school assure that the competence of each employee is adequate for current and future needs? What evidence is there that the school manages the work environment for promotion of motivation, satisfaction, development, and performance of its employees?

Data and Information

The quality system should be designed to ensure that accurate and appropriate data are easily available for fact-based decision making.

What evidence is there that relevant data are obtained regarding satisfaction of all parties for analysis for improvements? How are data obtained on learning and supporting processes for analysis for improvements? What evidence is there that self-assessment of the quality management system is used for improving the system's overall effectiveness and efficiency? How does the school control nonconformities? What evidence is there that the school analyzes nonconforming processes for learning and improvement? How does the school identify major trends? How does the school control its measuring and monitoring to ensure that correct data are being obtained?

System Design

The quality system should be designed to satisfy the students and stakeholders by having students take responsibility for their own learning processes, meeting the objectives and requirements of the curriculum, and providing support services that address needs and expectations.

What evidence is there that the school defines learning-related processes to ensure consideration of student needs? How has the school defined stakeholder-related processes to ensure consideration of needs? What evidence is there that the school has defined design and/or development processes to ensure consideration of student's needs? What evidence is there that related activities such as reviews, verification, and validation are addressed in design and/or development processes?

Supplier Partnerships

The quality management system should ensure that suppliers are aligned with the school's quality policy and objectives. What evidence is there that the school has defined purchasing and partnership processes to ensure consideration of needs? How are purchasing processes administered to include supplier's qualification to meet needs? What evidence is there that quality-related purchasing activities are subject to control, verification, and validation?

Improvement

The quality management system focuses on prevention and improvement based on trends to increase the effectiveness and efficiency of the school. What evidence is there that the school uses corrective action for evaluating and eliminating recorded problems affecting its performance? How does the school use preventive action? What evidence is there that the school uses systematic improvement approaches, methodologies, and tools to improve its performance?

Leadership

The quality system should be designed to identify leadership roles for managing the processes, measuring improvement, and taking corrective and preventive action. These roles can be played by many people within the school, but some cannot be delegated and are the responsibility of senior managers.

What evidence is there that the K–12 school's senior leaders set directions and create a student-focused, learning-oriented climate with high expectations? How are the directions, values, and expectations balanced among the needs of all students and stakeholders? What evidence is there that the leadership ensures the creation of strategies, systems, and methods? How do the values and strategies guide all the school's activities and decisions? What evidence is there that leaders inspire and motivate all teachers and staff and encourage them to develop learning processes? How do senior leaders serve as role models for leadership, commitment, and initiative?

Answering these kinds of questions helps the K–12 administrators plan the time and resources needed to establish and maintain a credible quality management system. The following example describes how seven Florida K–12 schools took the first steps toward a quality management system.

THE FLORIDA EXPERIENCE

Developing a mature quality management system for school districts requires time (often a decade) and a sustained commitment. In 1990, the Florida State Legislature voted to initiate a project to develop such a school improvement initiative under the title of Schoolyear 2000 (SY2000). Florida State University was selected to manage the initiative, using its own personnel, representatives of the seven participating school districts, and outside consultants. The initiative had well-developed concepts, a well-funded proposal, and seven school districts serving as test sites for the application of quality methods. The project managers embraced a system management philosophy. The school districts were not quite as committed, but agreed to participate.

One representative from each of the seven school districts was appointed to a quality system design team. The members included two information systems managers, several special education curriculum specialists, some assistant superintendents, and a quality manager. As a team they had responsibility for the personnel, equipment, and information systems in their districts and were oriented toward achieving a common quality system for all districts. Their schools had demonstrated an ability to absorb new ideas and make them work within existing programs. Their district policies contained some of the key system elements of a management system.

Mission

These schools established as their common mission, "All students will acquire the basic skills and competencies to succeed in the information age." "All students" included those with special needs for access to learning. The "basic skills and competencies" were those developed by the U.S. Department of Labor through the Secretary's Commission on Achieving Necessary Skills and Competencies (SCANS).

Scope

The scope of the Schoolyear 2000 quality system included all aspects of the school, including curriculum, instruction, assessment, staff performance and support, management and logistics, and student and family services. There were also basic elements of a quality system that were not considered. The most critical was the failure to define processes and to flowchart them. The quality assurance necessary to instill confidence in the students and stakeholders had not been considered. The significance of requirements for internal quality audits, corrective action, preventive action, and quality control was not understood as it applied to K–12 schools. Finally, there was no evidence of a clear idea of how to develop their quality system and how to introduce it into the seven school district test sites.

Recognizing that many basic elements of a quality system were not being addressed, experts in the area of quality were consulted. These experts recommended that a model (ISO 9001) provided by the international standards organization (ISO) be used. The recommended model, Model for Quality Assurance in Design, Development, Production, Installation, and Servicing, was, however, difficult to use because it was written for manufacturing organizations. As a result, it was thought desirable to develop an interpretive version of the ISO model for use in the educational field. This was done in 1996 and issued as ANSI/ASQC Z1.11—Guidelines for the Application of ISO 9001 to Education and Training Institutions or "Z1.11."

In addition to the Z1.11 standard, the school districts utilized information from the U.S. Malcolm Baldrige National Quality Award, which contains some of the fundamentals of Z1.11 and adds a lot more of what is often termed "world-class quality" considerations. Among these are emphases on leadership and strategic planning as well as customer satisfaction. In addition, some total quality management (TQM) tools were incorporated into their Z1.11-based quality system. Among them were the use of teams, the discipline of continuous quality improvement, and the development of customer satisfaction surveys. As a result, the following plan was devised to implement a generic quality system that could be tailored to the special needs of each of the seven school districts.

Getting Started

The first and most critical step was to ensure that all school districts' principals or superintendents were personally committed to the changes necessary for success, and were prepared to become the local champions of this concept. Their support was absolutely essential to sustain the work of others—the school administrators, teachers, and staff who would do the work of writing the detailed procedures.

The most effective commitment was made by one of the seven superintendents who said, "I will not discuss any procedural issue without a flowchart of that process." Knowing this, every administrative action was supported by a process documented by a flowchart. This superintendent's simple statement dealt effectively with individuals or groups who might have otherwise opposed a systems orientation. This example illustrates how, with a superintendent's operational commitment, process improvement can succeed.

Process Identification

Once the mission had been accepted, an end date was set for the introduction of the quality system. With this end in mind, processes supporting the mission were identified and flowcharted throughout each of the seven school systems. These processes were mutually supportive of the overall mission. Each district contributed additional personnel to the project team for developing the quality system.

The participating districts gathered processes from existing documents for each of the 20 elements of the ISO 9001 standard. Using the multifunction team led by the project manager with outside help from a consultant, a thorough examination of the current processes for each element in the standard was conducted and the findings were documented. In some cases, they found that they did not formally address the section of the standard but had some practice that could be adapted to fit the standard. These practices were listed. In other cases, they found that they had a formal process that fit or required some modification to be fully compliant with the standard.

The Gap Analysis

Once the self-assessment was complete, they were able to highlight the gaps between what they were currently doing and what they found needed to be addressed for full compliance. The team members were then organized into smaller groups, each of which accepted the responsibility for developing what was needed to make an element of the existing system fully compliant with the standard. The gap analysis identified certain critical aspects of the standard that were not currently addressed. As noted above, these included design control, process description and control, document control, corrective and preventive action, and internal quality audits. When the analysis was complete and assignments had been made, they established mutually agreed-upon schedules for draft process document completion by the scheduled end date set in step two (allowing for a thorough design review by the project administration).

One other major gap was found that was not covered by the requirements of ISO 9001. It was agreed that for each new or revised process, one or more measures of effectiveness should be developed and incorporated into the draft process description. This proved to be of great value when the process was discussed with the people involved in the process. Too often, the measures of effectiveness are left up to the people doing the work and intended goals are not reached.

Once the process was documented and approved as the result of design review, it was tried out. A key consideration for the tryout effort was that everyone who took part in or was affected by the tryout was effectively trained in what was changed and what was new.

The tryout also included a test of the selected measurement mechanism to determine whether intended results were achieved in addition to finding what may have needed changing in the new process. The approved process documentation was issued after revisions were made because of poor use of time, ineffectiveness, or misorientation of the process.

It was understood by all that it was important that practices and documentation match. Thus, there had to be a documented control process to provide the mechanics for such matching as well as both internal auditing and corrective action functions to ensure that any differences were detected and corrected. These and other controls were mentioned above as gaps found in the analysis. As indicated, they are provided for in ISO 9001 and, in fact, are necessary parts of any systematic approach to management of any function.

Once the process was tried, corrected as indicated, and ultimately approved, it was then seen to be necessary to train everyone involved. As much as practicable at any given time, this training covered the entire system—at least as far as it was developed up to that point. Training classes were needed to emphasize the role each group played so that everyone in the district was kept up to date on the progress being made.

The intent of this approach was to reinforce continuously that the system elements were (as they needed to be) interactive and intersupportive.

Results

The expected result of this quality system initiative was to produce a quality manual to guide the development of the system. If a manual could not be written then the systems approach would be difficult, if not impossible, to implement. The development of a quality management system would then be a failure.

It was at first thought that a manual could be fashioned after some examples from business and industry. This proved to be extremely difficult. At that time, there were no K–12 schools that had written quality manuals. Without such a manual it would be difficult to find a third party willing to register the system to ISO 9001 and the initiative would not be credible in the eyes of the student or stakeholder.

Several attempts were made to find examples of quality manuals from noneducation organizations. While some promised to share their manuals, none did. It turned out that these quality manuals contained details of processes that the organization wanted to remain secret for fear of losing a competitive advantage. The manuals were simply too valuable to share. An alternative way to create a credible quality manual needed to be found. This alternative was found in the data flow diagram that was created for the electronic support system design. It included 119 processes, 29 of which were also quality management systems processes. All processes were numbered and flowcharted with an accompanying narrative statement. They were all approved by the seven school districts, and were linked to the 29 processes in the quality system manual.

The following examples illustrate the process narratives developed for the Florida Experience as they related to the quality principles.

Student and Stakeholder

The skills and competencies mentioned in the mission statement were validated for Florida based on interviews with 625 job experts in 183 local organizations. In addition, a number of college and university students were interviewed to determine whether the skills and competencies applied to success in higher education as well. The data confirmed the validity of the skills and competencies for work and for higher education in Florida. Following this study, the State Chambers of Commerce spent a year attempting to expand the 37 SCANS Skills and Competencies and concluded that no additions were justified. The seven school districts accepted this mission, which remained unchanged for the duration of the initiative.

The stakeholders' needs were established in a community to serve as a confidence baseline. The approach used was developed by a customer satisfaction consulting company, and was described by John Goodman in 1992. Each question addressed a specific transaction for which someone in the K–12 school had responsibility. Where dissatisfaction was encountered, referral was made to the corrective action system in the school. A tracking system was established to follow up on the effectiveness of the corrective actions. The survey results provided useful information on what communities expected from public schools and how communities expressed their requirements.

The Sample

A 106-item baseline survey instrument was mailed out to a random sample of 14,995 parents with children enrolled in St. Lucie, Florida, public schools. An 18 percent return rate provided a 95 percent confidence level (±3 percent). The instrument included items designed to measure the community members' dissatisfaction with the functions and services provided by schools. Included in the survey were items that addressed transportation, safety, discipline, classroom activities, communication, problem resolution, and the school's ability to meet individual student needs.

Results

Four clusters of stakeholders' requirements made it possible for a school to identify and to meet stakeholders' expectations. A description of the four clusters follows.

The first cluster (or area), Personal Treatment, identified 33 percent of the stakeholders' needs and expectations. It included courtesy, respect, professionalism, responsiveness, and knowledge, in that order. The stakeholders' view of school service was based on specific events such as phone calls, community conferences, and Parent-Teacher Organization meetings.

The second area, Supervised Activities, explained an additional 17 percent of the stakeholders' needs and expectations to be assured that appropriate activities were being conducted by qualified adults. The major interest was in classroom activities, but counseling and playground activities were of concern as well.

The third area, Communication, explained an additional 5 percent of the stakeholders' needs and expectations. The stakeholders wanted to receive written communications they could understand and to be able to reply meaningfully about their concerns.

The fourth area, School Conditions, explained the remaining 3 percent of the stakeholders' needs and expectations. The remaining 42 percent was explained by random variation.

When community members visited the school, they wanted to see a safe, clean school with someone clearly in charge of whatever activities were going on at the moment.

Stakeholders did not visit schools very often. When they did, they expected to find the same service provided that they experienced in any retail or service organization. They expected to be treated as customers and were able to say, in a general way, what those expectations were. Schools wanted more specific expression of concerns so they could fix problems. However, stakeholders, like other customers, are sometimes uneasy about specifics, primarily because they understand and respect the teachers' professional position. A second reason communities keep comments general is the desire to have preventive action taken to improve the whole system and not to have their concerns quickly answered only to have them recur.

Learning and Supporting Processes

Several quality management system processes were developed to ensure that student and stakeholder requirements were met. An example of a process is presented below to illustrate that learning and supporting processes were controlled and improved. One example of these processes is included in each of the following quality principles.

Process #9 Establish Learning and Supporting Tolerances. The quality management system established tolerances for student and stakeholder requirements. These were developed from the surveys of skills and competencies (SCANS) and the stakeholders' requirements from the survey. The tolerances were expressed in terms of standard deviations, with results falling outside the specified number of standard deviations identified as being out of control.

Empowering People

A personnel database was established that included the processes for which all employees were qualified and their quality responsibility for each process. When responsibilities are clear and job descriptions are related to specific processes, employees are empowered to complete their tasks in a professional manner. Initially, there was concern that the employees' union would object to this process. Quite the opposite occurred. The union not only endorsed the process, but contributed a half-time staff member to be sure the activity had adequate resources for success. The union leadership believed that the process enhanced the professionalism of its members.

Process #19 Define School Employees Responsibility and Training. The senior management defines the number and level of employees in the school, the job description for each position, the associated responsibilities, and the training requirements. The database links each process with the human resources necessary for effective and efficient operation of the process. Improvement occurs when more employees are assigned responsibility for processes for which they have been adequately trained.

Data and Information

Information services provided data and information needed to operate an effective quality management system. A data flow diagram was prepared to ensure that all data collection, processing, and analyses were performed and controlled.

Process #37 Data Collection Instruments and Procedures. By request, suppliers, school districts, or agencies were provided instruments for collecting data regarding stakeholders' requirements—including surveys and focus group procedures. The database stores information on data collection instruments and on procedures for using the instruments. Data from the instruments can be returned to the database for analysis.

Process #44 SY2000 Records Advice. A Policy Advisory Committee, composed of key personnel from the seven test sites, business leaders, and state education leaders advises the SY2000 design team leaders on areas of design and controversial implementation of data and decision making. The process yields a flow of information and data advice.

System Design

The design of the quality management system needs to establish a quality policy, a quality manual, and the procedures for review of the system. The system needs to make system correction and to prevent results that are not consistent with requirements.

Process #21 Define Contracts, Suppliers, Customers, and Procedures. In this process, senior management defines the conditions under which suppliers provide goods and services to the school. The definition includes documented procedures for the control of verification, storage, maintenance, and servicing of goods and services.

Supplier Partnerships

Supplier partnerships are established to ensure that reliable and valid materials and equipment are available, effective, and appropriate for use in the classroom and for supporting services. Records of satisfactory delivery, billing, and service are maintained to evaluate the mutual satisfaction of the school and its suppliers.

Process #32 Establish Product Inventory and Procedures. The process is at the interface between administration and teachers or staff members. The purchasing department provides the quality system with a list of products via the process of establishing a product inventory. The product user provides information on satisfaction or dissatisfaction with the product or service. The information is stored in a supplier evaluation file and is available for subsequent purchases.

Improvement

Improvement is a continuous activity of the quality management system. Corrective action can be taken after problems are identified. Preventive action can occur before problems are encountered in the classroom or in the supporting services. The management of improvement resides with senior management to ensure that resources are available and that improvement supports the mission.

Process #10 Evaluate Student and Stakeholder Satisfaction. Input on students acquiring necessary skills and competencies and stakeholders' satisfaction with clusters of concerns was received from the database containing student records and results of surveys. Data were compared against tolerances. When the results fell outside the tolerances, then the entries became an input to the corrective and preventive action processes.

Leadership

Senior management reviews all aspects of the quality management system to balance the allocation of resources; to ensure that processes are carried out as designed; to assure continuing support of the mission; and to avoid duplication with other processes.

Process #23 Conduct Audit Results Review. In this process, the quality management system personnel meet with senior management to request an audit results review. Products, suppliers, and contracts are examined for problems and flaws in the system. After the review is completed, change requests and issues generated are recorded. The record activates the corrective action process to address the problem.

SUMMARY

The movement toward formal quality approaches in schools and school systems has been under way for several years. Local schools and school systems have adopted concepts of total quality management (TQM) and other approaches, with varying results. In 1990, the Florida State Legislature voted to initiate a project to develop such an approach to be accomplished by and under the title of Schoolyear 2000. Florida State University was selected to manage the project, using their own personnel, representatives of the seven participating school districts, and outside consultants. Over five years much was learned in attempting to apply ISO 9001 to the districts.

CONCLUSION

Many important things were learned from the Schoolyear 2000 experience. The two most important provide a conclusion for this chapter. First, if a K–12 school develops a quality system by itself, the above training should be provided to the key school district personnel, as well as members of the school board. If the entire school system (or a significant portion of it) develops the quality system, then not only the school board members, but also key political and higher education figures in the community, should be involved in the training sessions or, in their case, in sessions tailored for their purposes. This finding is supported by Bob Bowen in his work with Lancaster County, Pennsylvania, school system (see Chapter 5). Bob said that most of his effort went into keeping the school board committed for the five years it took to prepare for ISO 9001 registration.

Second, it is important for the leaders of the system effort to recognize that what they are undertaking, if successful, will have significant effects on the community as a whole. For this reason, involving key personnel from outside the K–12 operations can be a major factor in a successful effort that will survive the passage of time and the loss of initiating personnel. Some years ago, Madison, Wisconsin elected a new mayor. As his first action as mayor, he decided to focus on the "bottomline" and to gut the city's quality system. He met strong public opposition and wisely reversed his course, from then on strongly supporting that system. He discovered, as many others have, that once public institutions have adopted a "quality systems" mentality, there is no turning back.

ABOUT THE AUTHOR

Frank Caplan is an American Society for Quality Fellow, recipient of ASQ's distinguished Service Medal and of the ASQ Eugene L. Grant Award for education. He is the President of Quality Sciences Consultants, Inc., co-founder of National Educational Quality Initiative, author of *The Quality System*, and Editor-in-Chief of *Quality Engineering*.

9

Successful Applications

The success of a school's quality management system can be estimated from scores on self-assessment instruments for the Baldrige Criteria (maximum 1000 points) and ISO 9000 requirements (maximum 135 points). Additional internal measures of success may include the effectiveness of students' learning processes; the match between knowledge, skills, and behavior of the current school employees compared with process requirements; and survey results showing the local community's satisfaction with its schools. Successfully maintaining a quality system may include evidence of the leader's conviction under adverse conditions, the number of continual improvement cycles showing improvement, and evidence that administrators accept problems as opportunities for improvement.

Sometimes school administrators continue their commitment because of one or two critical quality system elements. For example, one superintendent found that discussions of process problems were more productive when a process flowchart was available to all participants. Another superintendent, who had registered several schools to ISO 9001, said, "If the school's quality system doesn't produce continually improved customer satisfaction results, I wouldn't give you a nickel for it."

Opinions on critical elements differ among the authors of this book. Each has personal views based on successful quality systems elements that worked best in their own districts, the expectations of parents who visit their schools, and their differing experience with objective evidence—which they all found elusive.

What follows is a composite of the authors' expectations when visiting schools based on their chapters. Readers may wish to compare this composite with their own expectations from school visits. The authors look for evidence that the eight quality management system principles have been successfully applied. There are also processes which the authors would not look at because the topics are outside the bounds of a basic quality management system.

In visits to classrooms, the authors would expect to find process control data, performance measures, and demographic data used for counseling students. The data would be based on facts—reliable, consistent, standardized, timely, current, accurate, and available. Records would also be readily available to make comparisons and examine performance trends. Teachers would provide graphic displays during meetings with parents.

Visits with support personnel would include demonstrations on how processes were continually monitored to detect causes of deficient administrative practice or processes that were unrelated to students' needs. Control charts would be used for process monitoring and improvement resulting in low inventory levels, minimum time between orders and delivery of school supplies and equipment, and a maintenance schedule that allows rapid responses to emergencies. Flowcharts would display the relations among the work of administrators, support staff, and teachers. Objective evidence would be provided on continual improvements that had reinforced public confidence in schools as community assets. When visiting the school's support services, the authors would not discuss efficiency, budget processes, or financial accounting practices.

School leaders would discuss how they meet their review responsibilities, how they monitor data points for the most frequent difficulty, and how they look for evidence of effective corrective and preventive action. Teams would have been used to analyze in-process data and to recommend what needed to be done next. Leaders would be expected to use objective evidence to determine what system changes are needed, to address system failures aggressively, and to eliminate them. The authors would not discuss leadership style, school culture, or the validity of the school's vision, mission, and objectives.

It would be interesting to the authors to know how the school meets parents' requirements for a safe school in a clean environment, communicates so they can understand, ensures respectful treatment, and provides qualified people doing appropriate things. The school might show the authors how the community views the school plans to meet the increasingly sophisticated requirements of the workplace. There may be evidence that improvements have ensured the community that an appropriate basic education is responding to community needs.

The authors would expect all employees to know the school's quality policy and to be able to relate the policy to their own responsibilities. Employees would participate in internal quality audits and understand the broader perspective this provides. Interviews might be held with employees who operate the corrective action system, learn how they identify critical problems, and what solutions they propose.

The authors would like to see how the school ensures that all employees are qualified to meet their responsibilities and the requirements of the tasks assigned to them. They would not expect to see the processes for negotiating union contracts.

Partnerships with other education agencies and service providers might be working together on an assessment-driven curriculum. Partners might work with the school toward common goals for productive citizens who can address complex problems under constantly changing conditions. Local businesses and industries might be helping the school establish and maintain its quality management system, supporting its standards-based instructional program, and providing guidance on continual improvement. The authors would not be interested in partnerships entered into for the purpose of raising the school's revenue.

Continual improvement is a noble goal for all schools and the authors would like to see the number of plan-do-check-act cycles used for all schools' improvement processes. Any objective evidence of reduced variability in processes and in process measures that moved performance closer to the requirement over time would be of interest. Quality tools might be used by students to improve their own learning processes. This would include individual study plans for continual improvement supported by the school's leadership. Data would be effectively collected and analyzed in a timely manner to provide immediate feedback to students. They would not expect to see attempts to make improvements on processes that were not stable and capable.

Finally, the authors would like to review the quality systems training provided to key school district personnel, to members of the school board, and to key figures in the community. Students' progress measurements would show where students are in their learning process and not how long they have worked on objectives. The quality system would provide the framework for aligning the school's vision, mission, curriculum objectives, support requirements, performance goals, lesson plans, supporting processes, students' performance evaluation, feedback to students, guidance for improvement, and related resource allocation. The authors would not expect to see slogans urging everyone to improve, undocumented claims of improvement, nor pledges to strive to improve.

As time goes on, the authors will expect more and more successful applications in K–12 schools. This will include higher expectations for results and innovation. In the end, the word "quality" should disappear as quality criteria, standards, and requirements become accepted school practice.

Index